£2.50

HEIR OF ADVENTURE

THE " ARMATA " AT LIVERPOOL, 1814

Heir of Adventure

The story of Brown, Shipley & Co.

Merchant Bankers

1810   1960

" A Worthy Merchant is the Heir of Adventure . . . His study is number, his care his accounts, his comfort his conscience, and his wealth his good name . . . . ."

NICOLAS BRETON
1545-1626.

By
AYTOUN ELLIS

ISSUED PRIVATELY BY
BROWN, SHIPLEY & CO. LTD.,
FOUNDERS' COURT, LOTHBURY,
LONDON, E.C.2.

PRINTED IN ENGLAND BY
BURRUP, MATHIESON & CO. LTD.,
CRANE HOUSE, LAVINGTON STREET,
LONDON, S.E.1.

To all those, in this and other countries, who have contributed to the progress of Brown, Shipley and Company.

THE HEIR OF ADVENTURE

A worthy Merchant is the Heir of Adventure, whose hopes hang much upon the Winds.

Upon a Wooden horse he rides through the World, and in a Merry gale makes a path through the seas.

He is a discoverer of countries and a finder-out of commodities, resolute in his attempts and royal in his Expenses.

He is the life of traffic and the Maintenance of trade, the Sailors' Master and the Soldiers' friend.

He is the Exercise of the Exchange, the honour of Credit, the observation of time, and the understanding of thrift.

His Study is Number, his Care his accounts, his Comfort his Conscience, and his Wealth his good Name.

He fears not Scylla and sails close by Charybdis, and having beaten out a Storm rides at rest in a harbour.

By his sea gain he makes his land purchase, and by the Knowledge of trade finds the Key of his treasure.

Out of his travels he makes his discourses, and from his Eye-observations brings the Model of Architecture.

He plants the Earth with foreign fruits, and knows at home what is good abroad.

He is Neat in apparel, Modest in demeanour, dainty in diet, and Civil in his Carriage.

In sum, he is the pillar of a City, the Enricher of a Country, the furnisher of a Court, and the Worthy Servant of a King.

NICOLAS BRETON.

1545—1626.

ACKNOWLEDGMENTS

As no text-book is available on the complex subject of Merchant Banking, my task in writing the history of Brown, Shipley & Co. would have been an impossible one had it not been for the ready help I received from the directors and staff—not forgetting those who are now in retirement. I also acknowledge the debt I owe to John Crosby Brown of New York whose history of the firm— "ONE HUNDRED YEARS OF MERCHANT BANKING" (1909)—proved to be a mine of information; also to his son, Thatcher M. Brown, whose private memoranda carried that story a stage further. In addition, the histories of Alexander Brown & Sons, Baltimore, and of Brown Brothers & Co., Philadelphia, have been most useful to me in my researches. I also wish to thank Lady Collet for giving me access to private papers of the late Sir Mark Collet that concern his long association with Brown, Shipley & Co.; also the librarians of the Institute of Bankers and the City of Liverpool for their help.

A.E.

CONTENTS

LIST OF ILLUSTRATIONS

LIST OF ILLUSTRATIONS—*continued*

Facing Page

INTRODUCTION

THE year 1960 marks the 150th anniversary of the foundation of Brown, Shipley & Company, Merchant Bankers. Although, in the City of London, there are several institutions much older—though not all in the same field—there can be few with a more romantic history.

The story begins with a Belfast linen-merchant, Alexander Brown, who emigrated to America during the Irish troubles at the end of the 18th century, establishing himself in Baltimore as an importer of Irish linens and other manufactured goods. Aided by his four sons this merchant venturer prospered. He built his own ships to carry his goods to the Southern States and sent them back laden with cotton and tobacco for Liverpool and Continental ports. Two of his sons were sent out to open branches in Philadelphia and New York; a third son remained in Baltimore to assist his father; the fourth and eldest son, William Brown, established himself in Liverpool as a merchant in 1810 and it is with him that this story is chiefly concerned.

On both sides of the Atlantic the Browns quickly gained an enviable reputation for integrity, stability, and unquestionable security, and thus were able to lend their name to accept or guarantee the bills of smaller merchants, enabling the latter to sell or discount their bills in the Money market at a rate they otherwise could not have secured. As the import and export trade expanded, the Browns found this credit banking and foreign exchange business developing so rapidly and to such an extent that, in course of time, they sold their ships and ceased to trade as merchants, concentrating solely on merchant-banking.

From the outset they have always been pioneers. They were issuing Circular Letters of Credit to customers before other American and English houses had entered the field. They pioneered the building of the Baltimore and Ohio railroad; they were the principal shippers of cotton for the Lancashire mills; and they played a leading part in the financing of trade between this country and America from the days of the Napoleonic Wars.

The firm weathered the storm of crisis after crisis on both sides of the Atlantic, and the story of how the name ' Shipley ' came to figure in the style or title of the firm is concerned with the great Panic of 1837 and is one of the most dramatic episodes in the bank's long history.

When the merchant trading days were ending and the time had come for Brown Shipley, as bankers, to open in London, they left behind them in Liverpool a tangible reminder of those pioneering days in the William Brown Library, the founder's gift to the city of his adoption. Since 1863 Brown Shipley have remained at historic Founders Court in Lothbury, within the shadow of the Bank of England.

Throughout the years Brown Shipley's bank has been the training ground for many who made their mark in the City. They provided the Bank of England with two of its Governors—Sir Mark Collet and Lord Norman— and among the trainees at Founders Court were many whose subsequent careers in commerce and in public life redounded to the firm's credit—notably the late Lord St. Just, and Lord Chandos. In the House of Commons, Colonel Clifton Brown (the late Lord Ruffside) was one of its most distinguished Speakers, and two of the Browns who were Members of Parliament—William Brown and his grandson, Alexander Hargreaves Brown—received baronetcies for their services.

To the general public the name of Brown Shipley is little known, despite the fact that an appreciable amount of the foreign currency they take with them on their travels abroad has probably reached them through Founders Court. To exporters and importers, however, Brown Shipley have long been recognised as a vital bridge in their transactions with overseas countries. The bank measures its own success by the multitude of successes it has helped to make, and every year added to its history increases its fund of goodwill.

Here is the story of a type of banking on which little has been written. It emphasises the importance of the personal element in business relations. Founded on the principle that character is more important than wealth, Brown Shipley's history reveals its willingness to suffer financial loss rather than tarnish its good name by one unworthy act. It is on that tradition of commercial honour and absolute fairness that the fortunes of the firm have been built up.

Since the First World War, Brown, Shipley & Co. and the American counterpart, Brown Brothers & Co.—now Brown Brothers, Harriman & Co.—which for over a century were one and the same firm, have gone their separate ways and more recently, in line with present-day requirements, Brown Shipley's private partnership of the past has given place to limited liability.

A century and a half of great adventure lies behind Brown, Shipley & Co. In that same tradition it " *plants the earth with foreign fruits, and knows at home what is good abroad* ", and as the " Heir of Adventure " will continue to make its contribution to British credit and to the high status of the City's banking system.

1810   1960

" *Trade is the Golden Girdle of the Globe.*"
WM. COWPER (1731-1800).

ALEXANDER BROWN & HIS FOUR SONS

Beneath the portrait of Alexander Brown (1764-1834)
GEORGE (left)   WILLIAM (standing)
JOHN A. (centre)   JAMES   (seated)

CHAPTER ONE

THE MERCHANT VENTURER

THE year 1798 was one of the most critical in Anglo-Irish relations. For generations past it had been England's policy—in Irish eyes—to suppress any movement that could result in Ireland's prosperity and freedom. In 1779 the Irish had won from Lord North a large measure of free trade abroad, but the heavy duties laid by the English Parliament on all Irish manufactures save linen and woollen yarn still shut them out of the English market. Six years later, Pitt, the apostle of free trade, decided on the economic freedom of Ireland and planned to make the British Isles a single fiscal unit; but this proposal proved unacceptable to the English House of Commons although it had at once been welcomed by the Irish Parliament. To all Irishmen of spirit, Presbyterian and Catholic alike, revolt was the one alternative to this oppression, and the war with France provided the opportunity. Wolfe Tone formed the United Irishmen movement and, in face of this danger signal, the Catholic vote was reluctantly conceded. Full emancipation was then promised to the Catholics by the viceroy (Fitzwilliam), who was promptly recalled for exceeding his powers, leaving behind him a country seething with bitterness and discontent. Meantime, fearful of full emancipation, the Ulstermen, predominantly non-Catholic, had reorganised the Orange Society. The civil disorders that followed, coupled with the organised revolt of the United Irishmen on the side of the French against the English, ending in the ruthless massacre of

1

thousands of the rebels at Vinegar Hill, prompted many Presbyterian Ulstermen to leave the country. Among them was a linen merchant named Alexander Brown.

Born at Ballymena, a centre of the Irish linen trade, he had built up a thriving business as a merchant, selling mainly to the Liverpool and American markets, and in addition he was one of several auctioneers to sell their linen from the tail of the wagon that had brought it into Belfast, or alternatively, to auction it in the Linen Hall in Belfast's Market Place. He had grown up in the Ulster countryside, where almost every cottage had its spinning-wheel or hand-loom and where every village green was a bleaching ground for linen. That Alexander Brown's business was prosperous, at least by the Irish standards of his day, is fairly certain, as he was able to send all his four sons to boarding-school in England. The school was at Catterick in Yorkshire and there is a family tradition that even if the fare it provided was not quite as spartan as at Dotheboy's Hall it had an equally astute Squeers as proprietor. The story goes that the headmaster promised the boys second helpings of pudding, provided they agreed to a minimum helping of the meat dish. As the stodgy pudding was cheap by comparison with the price of meat, he was thus able to cut the cost of feeding his pupils.

It was no easy decision for Alexander Brown to make when, in that critical year of 1798, he chose to leave Ireland. His eldest boy, William, had just left school at 16 years of age, but the three younger sons were still there. Apart from the effect on his business of the Irish revolt, the War with France had stopped the import of flax seed and potash, both essential to the trade. In any case, a country that appeared to be drifting rapidly to disaster was no place in which to bring up four sons. Leaving the younger boys at boarding-school he sailed for Baltimore with his wife and son William. There were good reasons for settling in that American port. An elder brother,

Stewart, had lived in Baltimore for 10 years and a brother-in-law had also been in business there, and Alexander had traded with one or both of them and through their letters had gained some knowledge of the place and the opportunities it offered. Both of them appear to have left Baltimore before the arrival there of Alexander Brown but this was no great problem to him as, all through life, it was what he knew rather than whom he knew that dictated his line of action. One of his maxims, and one he never tired of repeating to his sons in the years that followed, was " *Shoemaker, stick to your last* ". In beginning his career in the New World he naturally chose the same trade of linen merchant in which his experience and training could be used to the best advantage. It was a time when cotton goods were not the great staple of trade they were so soon to become. Linen goods of the better quality—and that meant, as it does to-day, Irish linen—were among the most prized possessions of the housewife fortunate enough to possess any.

When he had eventually settled down there duly appeared in the *Federal Gazette and Baltimore Daily Advertiser* of 20 December, 1800, the following announcement:

Irish Linen Warehouse,
No. 12 *North Gay Street.*
" *The Subscriber, lately arrived from Ireland, has brought with him a most complete assortment of* 4—4 *and* 7—8 *wide Irish linen which, upon examination will be found much lower than any inspected for three years past, and which will be sold low by the box or piece for cash or good acceptance in the city on the usual credit.*

Alexander Brown.
N.B. He has also imported and for sale three dozen very nice mahogany hair bottom chairs, made on the very best construction, and four eight-day clocks, which will be sold very low. 19 *December,* 1800 ".

Alexander Brown was back in business once again; and from this modest start there followed the swift expansion of his house and its development into what was to become one of the greatest business houses in the United States, its scope and influence constituting one of the real commercial romances of American history. The whole world was to be his province. Despite difficulties of distance and transportation he brought producer and consumer together. If there were no ships available he built them. If the producer had failed to find a market, he bought the goods and found the market. If credit was needed, he supplied it, and, without realising it, became the prototype in the New World of the merchant-bankers of 16th century Europe, and like the Fugger family in Germany who had dealt not only in goods but in money and news and even gossip from all parts of the world, it was Alexander Brown's concern, as the leading importer and exporter of his time, to know how, when, and where embargoes were laid and blockades maintained. It was equally important that he should know if honest and capable men were in control both in politics and finance in his own country and also in other lands with which he was doing business. In short, he eventually had his fingers on the pulse of world-trade, and this despite the fact that the only means of communication was by letter, carried in sailing-ships. His ships exported goods not only from Baltimore but from New Orleans, Charleston, Philadelphia and Savannah, and brought back the produce of Britain, France, Spain, and other countries. He kept himself informed of conditions and trends in every land with which he traded, and armed with the facts he would buy, sell, or hold on, as the situation seemed to demand.

When Alexander Brown died, in 1834, he left a personal estate of two million dollars; a great banking house the assets of which were far in excess of that figure; with all of his sons men of wealth in their own right. With the possible exception of J. J. Astor, no man of his time had left a deeper impression on the commercial life of America in the first half of the 19th century. In many ways these two were alike; both were world traders, had an intimate knowledge both of world markets and world politics, and used that knowledge as the basis of a judgment that enabled them to create in America its first great fortunes. Both had first landed at Baltimore, J. J. Astor as a penniless young man of twenty, Alexander Brown as a family man with sufficient means to start in business for himself. The younger Astor went north to New York and much of his great fortune was the result of investment in real estate; Brown's smaller but still considerable fortune was almost entirely derived from his trading activities.

The change from a strictly mercantile house to merchant-banking, rapid as it proved to be, was at first imperceptible. Beginning as an importer it was a logical development to be an exporter, and soon Alexander Brown's firm became one of the most prominent in exporting cotton and tobacco to England and the Continent. It was a natural evolution of these extensive import and export activities that an international banking business should be developed. No other American merchant had such a complete knowledge of the standing and credit of most English merchants as the Brown firm. Its name on bills gave them currency in the world's markets, and within fifteen years of landing in Baltimore his house had already a very considerable share of sterling exchange business. Conversely, Americans who wished to import goods, but whose reputation abroad was not sufficiently established to make purchases direct, were able to apply to Alexander Brown for credits.

Obviously no one man could alone have built up and controlled this international business. The clue lies in the style or title of the Baltimore house which, starting as " Alexander Brown ", had, within seven years, become " Alexander Brown & Sons ". It is the eldest of these four sons, William, who had accompanied his father and mother to Baltimore, with whom this story of Brown, Shipley & Co. is mainly concerned. Meantime, the three younger sons, George, John, and James, their schooling in England completed, had joined their parents in America, each, in turn, being initiated in the conduct of the business and trained to take his place in the family firm. In course of time, William was to establish himself in Liverpool; James in New York; John in Philadelphia; with Alexander Brown and his second son, George, at the parent office in Baltimore. In addition to these branches, agencies were established in Charleston, Savannah, New Orleans, and Mobile, and in each place the choice was the best man for the job that Alexander Brown could find.

The directing brain was that of Alexander Brown himself; the job of the others was to carry out his orders. Each worked separately and yet all together as a team, none knowing the full scope of the particular deal in those early years except the father and head of the firm. The old letter-books of the firm clearly show how he could marshal the resources of all those widely separated branches. He did the decisive thinking for them; he gave the orders, and the rebuke came swiftly and mercilessly when they failed to follow his instructions. He could not, however, have carried the burden alone. Behind him, all the time, was a woman of great character and indomitable courage—his wife, Grace. No great issue, no problem, no crisis arose without it being shared with her, and both husband and sons owed much to her cool judgment and sound commonsense. There was slight scope for initiative and originality as far as the sons were concerned, except for the one who was most like his father in character and temperament—the eldest son, William. In all the years during which Alexander Brown exchanged hundreds of letters with his sons, there are singularly few words of sentiment and affection on record, and yet no family could have been more closely knit; and when Alexander

Brown died, the sons were so broken up by his death that for a while the decision as to whether or not to continue the firm as a going concern was in the balance.

CHAPTER TWO

WILLIAM BROWN IN LIVERPOOL

ALEXANDER BROWN had given his son, William, a fine training. The reputation of the firm for honour, truth, and reliability was already established and freely acknowledged, and time and again (as correspondence shows) he had refused to do business, no matter how profitable the venture may have seemed, if he disliked or distrusted the principals concerned. " Let someone else engage in that line if they wish ", he wrote on one occasion, " but not Alex. Brown & Sons; nor will Alex. Brown & Sons have dealings with those who do." If, however, he liked and trusted a man, he did so completely. It was a deliberate policy with him, stressed over and over again in letters to his sons, to confine business alliances to the finest type and the most trustworthy of men. It was a policy that paid handsomely. In return, he insisted there should be absolute trust in those with whom the house was doing business, and the utmost generosity to them in all circumstances. Already the firm of Alexander Brown & Sons had become a tradition for reliability on both sides of the Atlantic and, in those uncertain days, very few if any American houses in the same field had such a fine reputation.

William had seen his father take the lead in every civic movement and had noted how the Baltimore community looked to him for support and guidance and how they respected his judgment. His father was, however, a difficult man and dogmatic to a degree. He held the reins, and he it was who dictated the road to be taken. As all four sons joined him in turn in partnership, he made it very clear that none was to be allowed much initiative in the conduct and development of the business as long as he was in command. Of all the sons William, being most like his father, had the same drive, the same initiative, the same ambition to succeed. He also inherited from his mother something of her shrewdness, courage, and personality and there were times when he stood up to his father and on occasion even challenged his judgment in certain transactions. This clash of personalities may well have been one reason, though it was by no means the only one, why William left Baltimore. A second reason was that of health. He was never robust and the American climate did not suit him, and there must have been many times when he longed for a sight of his native Ireland.

There was a third reason, and to Alexander Brown it was the deciding one for sending William across the Atlantic. Difficulties with England over the seizure of shipping had begun in 1804 and continued, with ever increasing bitterness, until the break came and the two countries were involved in the war of 1812. Until Nelson defeated the combined French and Spanish fleets at Trafalgar in 1805, both France and Spain had championed the rights of neutrals, but Bonaparte then declared the British Isles in a state of blockade and prohibited all commerce with them. All English merchandise was declared lawful prize, England retaliating by prohibiting any neutral ship from trading with any other European country, except Sweden, unless such ships first stopped in England or Ireland and paid a re-export tax. By this time the United States was one of the few neutrals of any importance. To add to the trading difficulties, the United States itself placed an embargo on all shipping in American ports. There were violent protests and threats of secession in the American South as shipping was brought to a virtual standstill. In 1809 the Embargo Act was repealed, but matters still went from bad to worse.

Alexander Brown was faced with a very tricky situation. As a neutral he had the choice of respecting the

French threat and to stop trading with England, or take the risk of seizure. As a merchant venturer in the old British tradition he took a chance. It is significant that no letter-books of the firm have survived, covering the period 1804-1810. It was probably considered far too dangerous to retain them, but later records confirm that during those critical years Browns were shipping cotton in increasing quantity to Liverpool, also tobacco and other goods, the cargoes being carried either in chartered ships or in the ships of Liverpool and Baltimore lines. As speed in transit became increasingly important if Browns were to be first in the market with the new season's crop, Alexander Brown built up his own fleet, and models of several of these ships are to-day among the historic treasures at the offices of Alexander Brown & Sons in Baltimore. It was vitally important to Alexander Brown to have someone like William on the spot in Liverpool, not only to keep him as fully posted as possible regarding the political and trading situation in Europe but also to ensure that his ships returned fully laden to America with the minimum of delay.

Perhaps, as events transpired, none of these was the real reason for William's journey after all; for when he reached his old home in Ballymena, in the summer of 1809, a boyhood romance with Sarah Gihon was revived and they married on New Year's Day, 1810, and crossed to Liverpool. Their first home there was at 3, St. George's Square, and before the end of the year, a daughter (Anne) was born. Meantime, William Brown had started in business under the name of William Brown & Company, the counting house being shown in Gore's Liverpool Directory as at 34, Strand Street. His main task at first was to look after the firm's shipments from and to the Old World, and his office was well placed near the waterfront. His business at first was virtually an agency for his father's firm and yet it was quite independent of the latter. To help him in Liverpool William Brown took as partner a cousin, William A.

Brown, then living in London. The business appeared to have been solely a shipping and merchanting business in its early days, but soon he was finding scope for an exchange and credit business that was to grow rapidly over the next few years.

The rise of Liverpool as a great port had been spectacular. In 1736, when the first direct shipment of cotton was landed in Lancashire, it was not to Liverpool that it came. At that time Liverpool was a mere village, with no facilities for handling such cargoes, the cotton being landed at a hamlet, 5 miles south-west of Lancaster, called Sunderland Point—not to be confused with the great seaport of the same name on the Durham coast. A Customs House and a small wharf and warehouses had been built, and a great future was predicted for this new port by those connected with the rapidly growing Cotton industry. No longer would they have to bear the expense and delay of transporting the cotton from the Port of London by the lumbering wagons—the " slow-coaches " that coined a new word in our language. Before long, however, the sandbanks of the river Lune, at whose mouth the little port of Sunderland stood, began to pile up higher and higher, making the approaches to the wharf both difficult and dangerous. It was soon evident that Sunderland's short life as the Lancashire cotton port was ended. It was then suggested that a " little place called Liverpool, farther down the coast " might be adapted as the cotton port. As for the miniature warehouses at Sunderland, they were converted into houses, and to-day the only remaining link between Sunderland Point and the cotton trade is the grave of a negro who had accompanied his master in 1736 when the first cargo of cotton was brought direct to this tiny Lancashire port.

A French traveller, Louis Simond, who visited Liverpool in 1810, says (in his " Journal ") that he had counted as many as " two hundred American vessels in Liverpool harbour ", representing, in his reckoning, " in

11

the article of cotton alone a trade worth annually two million pounds "; and yet only 20 years before, in 1790, when in New York, he says that he had been shown as something of a curiosity, the very first sample of Sea Island cotton. His estimate of the number of American ships lying at anchor is no doubt an extravagant one; all the same, the cotton trade was expanding at a remarkable rate, war or no war. Unlike the Port of London, where wharfinger and warehouseman are one and the same firm, Liverpool already had a very fine warehousing organisation second to none, some of its buildings being many storeys high. Several were of very recent construction, replacing older buildings which had been destroyed in disastrous fires. One of the worst fires was in 1802 in the Goree Piazza when seventeen warehouses were destroyed and damage to the amount of £320,000 was caused. This was the fire that brought to an untimely end the Liverpool St. George Fire Office, formed only four months previously and heavily involved in the disaster.

William Brown had spent a year in Liverpool as an independent house. It was important that he should return to Baltimore and give his father a first-hand account of political and trading conditions and to discuss with him and with his brothers the plans he had in mind for the expansion of the business in Liverpool. It was a time, as we have seen, when letter-writing could be dangerous or, at least, unwise. Such letters might have fallen into the hands of either belligerent or, with England and America likely to be at war with each other, it might conceivably have involved Alexander Brown or William himself in considerable difficulties. With this in mind, and naturally anxious to introduce his wife and baby Anne to his family, he took them with him to Baltimore, leaving his cousin, William A. Brown, to look after the small but growing business in his absence. It was while they were staying with his parents that war between America and England was declared.

Meantime, George Brown, who was to succeed his father as head of Alexander Brown & Sons in the years to come, had been visiting correspondents in Portugal, and word had been sent to him to make his way to Liverpool without delay and there await further instructions.

It was a great blow to Alexander Brown when war was declared with England. He, more than most Americans, knew the strength of the British fleet and the unpreparedness of his country for a struggle. New England generally was strongly opposed to war but the President, Thomas Jefferson, always friendly to France and with no love for England, refused to believe that there had been just as much interference, if not more, by the French with American shipping than by the English. As has so often been the case in more recent years, events in Europe were too remote to be understood in America, where few seemed to realise that the ruthless ambition of Napoleon must be curbed. Alexander Brown had optimistically expressed the opinion more than once that England would withdraw her Orders in Council, which prohibited American and other neutral ships from trading with Europe. " We have great hopes ", he wrote, " that the Prince Regent, when he comes into full power, will see it the interest of England to be on good terms with this country." The daily accounts of " the capture (and) burning of American ships by the French give some indication ", he sarcastically wrote, " of what might be expected from the great Emperor's friendship ". In the long talks he had had with his father, William discussed with him the many problems with which they would be faced if war should be declared, but neither of them really believed that a declaration was likely. As late as April, 1812, William was writing to William A. Brown in Liverpool:

" . . . The capture of several (American) vessels, lately bound for Spain and Portugal, by French Frigates, has caused the *National Intelligencer* to hold a language towards that nation very different to what it has been accustomed to do. It now admits that the lack of means alone is the reason why they have not captured more vessels than England, and that their continental seizures make their depredations on American property fully equal. From this and other causes I infer that we shall not have War, and would by no means hold produce for War prices where a discretionary power rests with us. In other cases, act by instructions; rather break the owners than break orders. If we act otherwise we will soon lose our business. I hope to be leaving by some route or other for England, and soon after, to see you and George in Liverpool . . . am still of opinion the chances are in favour of Peace."

That same month, in another interesting letter from Baltimore to William A. Brown, he wrote:

" . . . For the last 10 days very great activity has prevailed in this port in getting vessels off, by working day and night, and now there is a fleet beating down the river, against a head-wind, for fear of our Government keeping them at home. It is impossible to conjecture what will follow an Embargo, but it is highly possible it will cause a good deal of speculation in Liverpool, and may enable us to run of(f) the ordinary Tobacco. With respect to the other sales—I am quite at a loss what to say: you must act as you think best as it is difficult to know what to do. If war, produce will rise; if peace, the reverse may take place . . . I write by several conveyances that you may be on a footing with others and to prevent you being speculated on, yet am of opinion that unless you see from the attitude England is assuming that she means to commence the War, and that the United States will not strike the first blow, I do not think that America has any serious intentions of going to War . . . If the prices of Tobacco get up to 9d. or 10d. for leaf, and 11d. or 12d. for stemm'd, it would be desirable to sell freely . . . It occurs to me that if you see War is likely to take place, that a British Licence can be got for the *Armata* to carry provisions to Cadiz or Lisbon, or Naval Stores and Cotton to Liverpool, with the liberty to retain her American papers. If so, it would be desirable to send out a licence with all dispatch. You can consult George on the subject . . . but I still think it impossible that our Executive can have any serious intention of going to War with England in the unprepared state of this country."

Optimistically, and always with an eye to business, he went on:

" If the Non-importation act is removed, the orders for coarse goods, suitable for this fall (i.e. autumn) trade will be immense and they will get up rapidly in England. I should think it safe and good speculation for you, on receipt of this, to have Three or Four Thousand Pounds invested in those articles. If the intercourse should be opened when that news reaches England, it will be impossible to secure the goods, so many will be wanted."

A few days later he is again writing to William A. Brown in Liverpool but in less sanguine terms. " Better not make any purchases in expectation of removal of the Intercourse, but remain in Liverpool until my arrival. We shall then know better what new projects of business it will be advisable to pursue. Don't by any means touch Exchequer Bills or any kind of Government security. A War with a country would depreciate anything of that kind prodigiously." The War came; but it was far from bringing the business between America and England to a standstill. Three months passed and William was in New York, still trying to get a passage to Liverpool. In a letter of 22 June, 1812, we find Alexander Brown writing to William Cumming, the manager of the Liverpool office, admitting that he had been wrong in the advice tendered some weeks earlier:

" . . . It would have been well if pointed directions had been given William Brown & Co. to hold over part of our Tobacco; but the prevailing opinion was that the War measure would not be carried in the Senate. Indeed 4 days before we received the declaration large bets were offered that it would not pass; . . . the voice of the people was almost unanimously against War . . . Indeed such was our hopes and expectations that we were frequently, since the sailing of the last packet (boat), glad we had not given any positive directions to hold part on . . . but we could not bring ourselves to believe such a measure would be carried in the unprepared state of the country."

The War of 1812 was the first of many great financial crises with which Alexander Brown & Sons in Baltimore and William Brown & Co. in England were faced. It will now be seen how they rode the storm.

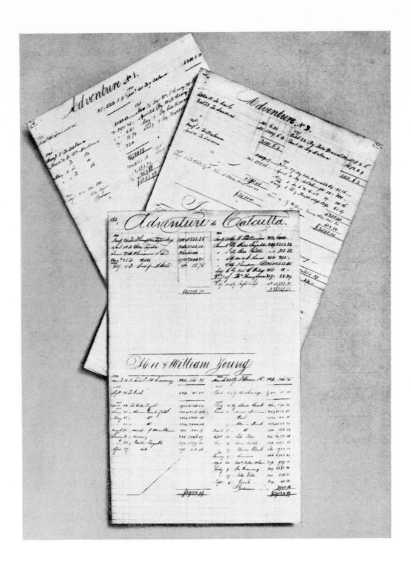

PAGES FROM ALEXANDER BROWN'S FIRST LEDGER

It is characteristic of the Browns that the first page should be
headed "Adventure No. 1". They were Merchant Venturers in
the best tradition.

WILLIAM BROWN'S MOTHER

Alexander Brown's wife, Grace, was a woman of great character.
She had a profound influence on the business in its early days
and on her four sons.

CHAPTER THREE

THE WAR OF 1812 AND THE CRISIS THAT FOLLOWED

AT the end of August, 1812, William Brown was fortunate in being able to get a passage from New York to Liverpool in the *Pacific*—the first cartel ship to sail after the outbreak of War. (The two countries, by " cartel " or agreement, were thus able to arrange for the exchange of prisoners.) William's wife accompanied him but their small daughter, Anne, remained behind with her grandparents in Baltimore. Awaiting William in Liverpool was his brother George (whom his father had made a partner in the Baltimore firm in 1808). George had been to Lisbon to meet their correspondent, Creighton, and to study trading conditions at first hand. His younger brother, John (who had also been made a partner in 1810, in place of William), was also in Liverpool, en route to Portugal. They were anxious days for the parents as most of their sons' letters home never reached their destination. In a letter to William, awaiting him in Liverpool, Alexander Brown tells him he had had no news from John for some considerable time and " had it not been for letters from Mrs. Dickey to Mrs. Robert Dickey in New York, we would still be ignorant to whom John is married, as no letters mention her name, and we have no word from John since he left Liverpool ". It appears that when John and his wife eventually sailed from Lisbon for Baltimore their ship was captured and taken into a West Indies port.

William Brown's first concern on his return to Liverpool was to examine the books and discuss with his

17

partner-cousin how things had gone in his absence. Such an unsatisfactory state of affairs was revealed that he decided to dissolve the partnership forthwith, and he wrote to his father outlining the reasons that led to this drastic step. In a letter to George, his father commented as follows: —

"I am truly sorry to find Wm. A. had acted in such a manner as to induce Wm. to dissolve the partnership, but I do not see how he could do otherwise. It would be such a weight on his mind to have a partner in whom he had not full confidence . . . still, it will give me great pleasure if the dissolution can be accomplished without making a family quarrel which, of all quarrels, are the most distressing."

Whatever had gone wrong appears to have been due solely to bad judgment, and it would seem that Alexander Brown was inclined to blame George, who was in Liverpool at the time, for at least part of the trouble. This concerned the selling of tobacco belonging to the firm at the low market price prevailing just as war was declared. In a further letter to George he says: "A moment's reflection should have told you that war would double and treble the price of tobacco. I am greatly disturbed and distressed over your action in selling."

There was a suggestion that John should join his brother William in partnership, taking the place of his cousin, but it is evident that, for the time being at any rate, William preferred to carry on alone, and it is very doubtful whether the volume of business in the first year of the war justified him taking a partner. William was at that time his father's agent and both had to play a waiting game until the war had ended. Alexander Brown had pointed out to his sons, before the American War had started, that there would be great opportunities for money-making, as blankets, flannels, wire, and other goods would soon be in short supply. He instructed George, in Liverpool during William's absence, to lay out three or four thousand pounds on such materials and hold them against a rise. With the same idea in mind, the Baltimore house was at that time dealing heavily in tobacco, flour, linen, dry goods, copper, tin, paint, and other commodities likely to be in short supply.

Throughout the War, Alexander Brown carefully studied the markets of the world. He it was who supplied the judgment and gave the orders, the sons merely carrying out instructions. Not that there were at first many opportunities of doing business, as he was always most anxious to comply strictly with all the war-time laws and conditions of his adopted country. For instance, he first consulted the American Attorney General before advising Wm. Brown & Co. to purchase an English (Board of Trade) licence for his ship, the *Armata,* en route to Lisbon. (She was the first of many ships the Browns were to own.) Being given an assurance " that there is nothing treasonable and improper " in using these licences, he suggested that William should try to purchase as many of them as possible, although his immediate concern was to see the *Armata* return home unmolested. Failing such a licence, he advised John, then believed to be in Lisbon, to sell the ship if he could get a good price for her or, alternatively to send her home (to Charleston) in ballast if peace was not declared in the meantime. Then came news that the British had stopped issuing these immunity licences, George being then told to weigh up the prevailing situation and use his own initiative in deciding the fate of the ship—one of the very few occasions on which a son was given a free hand. But he was in optimistic if cautious mood as he wrote:

" If the *Armata* gets safe to Lisbon and home again, not being insured, we cannot make less than 60 or 70 Thousand Dollars by this year's trade. Circumstanced as we now are, it would be wrong for us to run the risk of commencing any establishment or trade that could not be carried on without hazard."

Within a few weeks, however, British vessels had entered

Chesapeake Bay, put the frigate *Constitution* out of action, and had plundered and set fire to the villages of Frenchtown and Havre de Grace, thus disrupting the internal trade between Baltimore and Philadelphia. Writing to William (in May, 1813) he comments on the situation:

"... the state of alarm we are kept in by several British Ships of War being opposite the mouth of our River for some time ... If there was a depth of water, or if they had a sufficient number of land troops, they would no doubt pay Baltimore a visit. Great exertions are making to strengthen the Works and Forts round the Town, and numbers of militia are coming in from the country, which added to the Volunteers and militia of the city, must in a short time make the place too formidable to be attacked ... but the Banks have removed their specie to Frederick, and very many of the Dry Goods merchants are moving a considerable part of their goods into the country.

We have not yet moved anything, indeed we have only a few boxes of Linen and our houses and furniture that can suffer, and our bills receivable are of such a complexion that it is impossible to lose much of them, happen what will. Should the alarm continue, the family will move to the country."

After assuring William that his little daughter " is as well as you could wish her ", he laments " the state of things and not knowing well how to employ money with safety ".

It is clear from his letters of the period that Alexander Brown had turned much of his accumulated stock of goods into cash, the rise in prices that followed the Declaration of War having enabled the Baltimore house to sell to advantage. The same applied to William in Liverpool, and indeed where either of them could see an opportunity of earning interest on their money, provided there was no real risk, they were quick to seize it, as neither believed in money lying idle. For instance, when the report reached Baltimore that a negotiator had gone to Russia " to treat with Great Britain for Peace " he tells William that it " induced us to make a speculation in Exchange . . . in the enclosed bill £10,000 (in conjunction with P. E. Thomas & George), Six Thousand of which place to our credit and four to their credit ". He also says that " D. A. Smith is going to Phila.(delphia). We shall give him some bills if he can get a good Exchange to take advantage of it ". All the same, he was uneasy in his mind, feeling that he was " remitting rather more than intended ", but hoping that William could " continue to make Interest of them without risk ".

In almost all his letters to his sons he wrote as the firm and signed " Alex. Brown & Sons ". The only sentimental touch he permitted himself was to end his letters with such words as " Believe us, dear William, Your affectionate friends, Alex. Brown & Sons ". Even this was frequently abbreviated, " dear " becoming " d " and " affectionate " being cut to " aff.". It was, however, a closely-knit family, and when any of his sons were in peril, as for instance when one of them was on the high seas and raiders were known to be holding up shipping, his letters would reflect his anxiety and uneasiness, and it was at such times that he would drop the formal and somewhat brusque ending and sign himself " Your affectionate father ". Although no letters of Mrs. Alexander Brown have survived, it is probable that she furnished the gossip and more personal items of news to the scattered family. Indeed, she was " the power behind the throne " and her contribution to the fortunes of her husband and the firm was a considerable one.

When the War ended, the years that followed were among the worst ever experienced, and panic swept both the United States and England. Many of the oldest and strongest houses in New York, Philadelphia, and Boston crashed; but it was during this very period of financial stress and storm that the genius of Alexander Brown shone brightest. The depression was great and little money was being made in either country, but Alexander Brown had seen the storm coming and was ready for it. He had restricted his commitments with characteristic foresight; had buttressed more than one of his business friends with the soundness and strength of his own firm, and was able to keep his ships on the seas and his cargoes moving. That he suffered losses at times was not surprising; no man could guess right every time but few had that peculiar genius which enabled him, over and over again, to retrieve a mistake in judgment and turn it, in the end, to profit. Writing to his cousin in Ireland, in the spring of 1819, he was in pessimistic mood:

" Such is the state of things here that no one buys anything beyond his immediate need, be the article never so cheap. We cannot hope for anything here but loss, as our stock of goods is too heavy to force off at this time."

Yet, within a few days of this, he was in buoyant mood. He had invested very large sums in United States Bank stock, both personally and in his firm's name, and was a director of its Baltimore branch. He it was who discovered that certain officers and directors of the Bank were speculating in the stock—with the Bank's own money !—and led the fight to have them removed. Despite a loss of 3,600,000 dollars, it was largely due to Alexander Brown that the Bank was out of danger within a year. His association with this crisis in the affairs of the United States Bank established still more firmly his reputation and that of his House for honesty and integrity.

Already he had over 40 agents (or correspondents) of the highest standing in every centre of importance. His firm grew year by year, keeping pace with the development of the country as a whole, and on that same day, in 1818, when the foundations of the Capitol at Washington were laid, he opened a branch of Alex. Brown & Sons in Philadelphia, putting his son John in charge. As the firm had a virtual monopoly of the linen trade, it is not surprising that the following announcement of the opening of the branch should be concerned with linen:

" John A. Brown & Co. take this opportunity of informing those who have been in the habit of purchasing linens imported by Alexander Brown & Sons, of Baltimore, that the above firm is a branch of that concern and that both houses will import a constant supply of cheap linens."

This was at a time when, all around him, firm after firm was failing. They were (as he wrote to one of his agents in 1819) " times that require caution, and it is not worth while to run any unnecessary risk. A man is a fool to do so under these circumstances, unless his need is great. Ours is not ". To another agent he wrote:

" To give you a description of the state of public feeling in this place would be impossible. To give you a list of the failures equally so. The question is, who has not failed and who is solid enough to stand the strain. In comparison with the general distress, we have suffered little and we now hope the worst is over."

A month later, he was writing to a firm in New Orleans, through which Alex. Brown & Sons bought cotton for the Liverpool market:

" Entire confidence is restored in our banks, but individual distress still continues. Yesterday John and Adam Levering stopped. Whether this will be the cause of bringing down others I am unable to say."

Despite the crisis there was scarcely a year that did not show an increase in his firm's business and an improvement in Alexander Brown's personal estate. By 1820 his firm, having grown into a great trading house, had also become a really important banking house. In this development he had been assisted, to a marked degree, by his son William in Liverpool.

When the Anglo-American War had ended, in 1814, it

was decided to re-establish the Liverpool house, then trading as Wm. Brown & Co. (William being an independent proprietor), and to re-style it Wm. & Jas. Brown & Co. It was inevitable that William should be brought back into the family fold and that his firm should become the Liverpool house of Alex. Brown & Sons. A formal partnership was entered into by the four brothers, William, George, James and John. As the Brown capital in Baltimore was considerable, and this despite the large sums invested in United States Bank stock and the demands of his American business, Alexander Brown sent large funds to William. In spite of William's assurance that Wm. & Jas. Brown & Co. was " all right ", he still continued to send money to Liverpool, for, as he said by way of explanation, " When many of the first-rate houses in England are tottering and suspected, it is of the very greatest importance that W. & J. Brown & Co. should be perfectly easy in money matters. That is why we are sending you the additional 5,000 shares of United States Bank stock. There must be no feeling of uneasiness about us ". The only " uneasiness ", as far as William was concerned, was due to holding idle money. He looked around him for bills that were really safe to purchase—and they were the exception with the drain of specie from the banks of both countries continuing—and was not slow to make full use of any opportunity to employ his capital to the best advantage. He had to tread warily as in those earlier days his father—and his three brothers, too—did not always see eye to eye with him. Ten years in Liverpool had taught William a great deal—much more than one could learn in Baltimore—not only about the standing of English merchants and manufacturers, and particularly those concerned with a rapidly expanding cotton trade, but also about shipping and Britain's overseas trade. Nor was he content to rely entirely on the letters from Baltimore for information concerning the state of affairs in America and elsewhere. He made a practice of

24

encouraging the many captains of American ships, coming into the port, to make his office their headquarters. He had moved to 7, Union Court, Castle Street, keeping on (for a year or two) the original dock-side office in Strand Street. These sea-captains were, in most cases, owners of or part-owners in their vessels, many being well-acquainted with commercial affairs, and some being interested financially in their cargoes. It was his practice to entertain them regularly, and as his house was a modest one he did so at the Waterloo Hotel, on the site of which the Exchange Hotel now stands. It is said that the Waterloo Hotel was famed for its turtle soup, but it is much more famous as the birthplace of the Waterloo Cup, the blue riband of Coursing, initiated by the Earl of Sefton in 1836. Throughout the years the draw for this 64-dog contest has taken place each February, in its earlier years at the old Waterloo Hotel, and later at its successor the Exchange Hotel.

The next few years was a period of expansion and progress for both the parent firm and W. & J. Brown & Co. Both countries had left the crisis behind them and trade was booming, and by 1825 William found that he must have at the Liverpool house someone familiar with American business to help him. Choice fell upon Joseph Shipley, an American, at that time established in Liverpool as agent of John Welsh, a well-known merchant in Philadelphia.

CHAPTER FOUR

EXPANSION AND PROSPERITY

THE twenty years that followed the end of the War with France were wonderful years for the Browns. In Britain manufacturers had piled up vast stocks for export; industrial capacity was rapidly extending; much surplus capital awaited investment in America, and both nations had plenty of money to spend. The situation in Great Britain at that time was in many respects comparable to that in the United States after World War II. Men of enterprise, like William Brown, were not slow to exploit the opportunities offered. All over Europe there was a demand for British goods. There were also great opportunities for money-making in America, with its rapidly expanding economy, its great natural resources, its vast expanse of unexploited land, its confident and ambitious people, and—most important— a tolerably stable government. America's merchant fleet had even dared to compete with the British, and Alexander Brown's ships were among the many carrying raw materials to all ports of the world, particularly to Liverpool. These exports paid for finished goods from England and other countries. In many parts of the World there was political instability and consequent trading risks, and (in the words once used by Alexander Brown in a letter to William) " where the risks are too great . . . one loss may wipe out a hundred safe arrivals . . . You cannot make a mistake by being sure ". It was not solely a question of faith in a man's financial strength, there had also to be faith in his character. " Don't deal with people about whose . . . character there is question.

It keeps your mind uneasy. It is far better to lose the business " he counselled. William had more enterprise and initiative than his brothers and was at times inclined to be a bit headstrong. His father had to put the curb on him more than once; for instance, when he wanted to go into the insurance business; and again, when a big land speculation had attracted him. " The risks are too great and we know nothing about the business ", he wrote to William regarding insurance; and he dismissed the land speculation firmly with these words: " We are doing well enough as it is. Be content."

They were certainly doing well on both sides of the Atlantic. It was not unusual for Alexander Brown & Sons to deal in as many as 30,000 bales of cotton in one transaction, and soon the Browns were handling 75 per cent. or more of the American cotton, these huge shipments to Liverpool (and Havre to a smaller extent) being William's responsibility. He knew every cotton broker and manufacturer in Lancashire, and believing there was a great opportunity of making handsome profits from investment in certain Mills, he wrote to his father, strongly recommending this new departure, and seeking approval for investment in a Spinning Mill. The reply he received was a masterpiece of clear thinking and sound reasoning and ran as follows:

" Dear sir:

As our A. B. goes to Phila. tomorrow morning to attend the meeting of the Stockholders, Bank U.S., on 1 Nov., we answer your private letter of 9 Sept. before his departure that he may see it. We all agree in opinion it would be wrong and imprudent to embark in any other pursuit than that we are respectively engaged in, and although the amount you would have to advance now to become interested with Moore in the Cotton Mill for one of your children is not large, yet it could not be spared without resorting to the financiering business measure you point out, so long as we are such heavy holders of U.S. Bank Stock.

27

However profitable the business may be now, we know of none subject to more reverses than the Cotton Spinning trade, and becoming once interested, even in the name of your child, your capital, credit and resources would be called into action for the use of that establishment whenever it would be required; and when once it's known or even suspected that you are in any way interested in such an establishment, it would do injury to the credit of your house.

Look around you in Liverpool and see those Merchants who have so many concerns that they cannot superintend themselves, how, sooner or later, it does them injury if it does not ruin them altogether. Having too many things to attend to, it distracts your attention and draws it off from your regular pursuit. We don't think you need be anywise apprehensive of not having your share of business. We are not by any means advocates for a large one. A small business well-attended to is conducted with much more satisfaction and comfort, and if the capital is too large to be employed in it, let it be invested in stocks.

If we look round here we find that those persons who have kept steadily to one pursuit are far the richest men, and those who are interested with one and another in different pursuits, no matter how profitable they may be or appear to be at first, are always ruined sooner or later. We are therefore unanimously opposed to any interest being taken in the Cotton Mill.

In the management of one's business it is not only necessary to be correct, but not to be suspected of incorrectness. If you or any of your family were interested in a Cotton Mill and it became known, which must be the case, shippers of Cotton might conceive there was a risk if sent to you of it being sold to your own establishment lower than it ought. You know how such persons are always disposed to grumble and find fault on losing sales. But on the score of

Interest, without any other consideration, one business properly conducted is the surest and safest way to make money, and enables one to move with so much ease. The surplus funds can always be used with safety here to make 6 to 7 per cent. per annum and perhaps more."

There was to be no further question of Mill Shares for William Brown and his children in the face of such an uncompromising reply. Subsequent events in the Lancashire Cotton trade proved the soundness of the advice—that the cobbler should stick to his last; and yet Alexander Brown had himself been venturesome enough in his earliest years in Baltimore; indeed his first ledger opens with accounts headed "Adventure No. 1", followed by "Adventure No. 2"; but it was never a rash adventure on which he knowingly embarked. He bought anything that could be sold at a profit, and to him it was a great thrill to see his ships go out laden, to return with an endless variety of eminently saleable goods for the home market. In 1825, for instance, one of his ships, the *Sally*, took out its cargo of cotton to Liverpool, went on to Havre and Cadiz, and eventually returned home with a mixed cargo of coffee, pepper, sweet oil, indigo, and French wine and brandy, with fine champagne at 18 dollars per dozen and brandy at 2 dollars 30 cents per gallon—equivalent to 1s. 3d. a bottle!

Ships were not only a necessary adjunct to the Browns' business but an outlet for that spirit of adventure that had to be severely controlled in their day-to-day dealings. When Alexander Brown bought his first ship in New York in 1811 she was still on the stocks. This was the *Armata*, to which reference has already been made. He first put her in service between Baltimore and Liverpool and Belfast, primarily to carry his linens. The War changed his plans for her, and after taking cotton to Liverpool she loaded with provisions and other English goods and went on to Cadiz and Lisbon. Alexander Brown's pride in his first ship is reflected in the correspondence that has survived. For instance, to his nephew, William A. Brown, a partner in Liverpool at the time, he proudly describes his new acquisition:

" The *Armata* of Baltimore was built in N. York in the years 1810 and 1811, has two decks, three masts; her length is 108 f. her breadth 29 f. 6 in., her depth 14 f. 9 in. and measures 413 56-95 Tons; has round tuck; square stern'd Ship, with a billet head."

The *Armata* is pictured (frontispiece) arriving in the Mersey in 1814. The Liverpool skyline was very different from what it is to-day and only St. Nicholas's Church and the Town Hall behind it have survived. The huge American flag—the only one to have 15 stars and 15 stripes—was usually hoisted as the ship reached port and there is an interesting story behind it. Vermont and Kentucky had been admitted to the Union and Congress had added a stripe and a star to the National flag for each of them. This was the flag that waved defiantly over Fort McHenry when the British Navy attacked on the night of 13 September, 1814. Francis Scott Key was a hostage on the British frigate *Surprise* and his pride on seeing the American flag still flying on the Fort next morning inspired him to write " The Star Spangled Banner "—America's National anthem.

There was a signal station in those days in Baltimore, on Federal Hill, and as soon as an observer recognised (by its house flag) a particular ship coming up the harbour, he would promptly hoist a duplicate flag on his tower to give the owners their first news of her safe arrival. In their forty or fifty years as ship-owners, Browns had two designs for their flag, one being adapted possibly as a war-time expedient. This red, white and blue striped flag was later discarded for the original which had a white horizontal stripe on a red ground, with a large letter B in white, below the stripe. It flies to-day not only in Baltimore but also in New York, above the entrance to 59, Wall Street, home of Brown Brothers, Harriman & Co., as a visible reminder of those romantic days when the Browns first ventured into ship-owning.

That it was not all smooth sailing and a fair breeze is clear from the fact that in 1825, the very year in which the New York branch was opened (with his son James in charge), no fewer than three of Brown's vessels were lost. The little *Armata,* however, was more fortunate. After running the blockade and the countless hazards of War, she was in constant service until 1831, when she was sold to make way (with other old ships of Brown's fleet) for fast clipper-type vessels. It had already reached a period when time was the essence of the contract, and Brown's ships were to be among the fastest on the Transatlantic run until they were ousted by the steamship. It is interesting to note that the *Baltimore Gazette* of 11 August, 1828, reported the safe arrival of the *Armata,* laden with " salt, linens, and whiskey, and 165 passengers ". It seems unbelievable that this little ship of only 400 tons should carry such a load, but such was the case, and as proof that it was an enjoyable voyage, one of the passengers, writing 37 years later, says: " I look back with pleasure and clear remembrance to the appearance of our family group, seated on the deck of the old *Armata*—little girl that I was." For another 20 years this sturdy little ship was whaling. She was eventually wrecked on a reef near Cape North on 15 July, 1851, her cargo of 200 barrels of sperm oil and 4,500 barrels of whale oil being taken off before she was abandoned. It was a tragic end to Alexander Brown's first ship and had he been alive when it happened it is fairly certain he would have been incredulous, since he could never have conceived it possible for anything concerned with Alex. Brown & Sons to founder.

It was on 3 April, 1834, that Alexander Brown died. He had caught a chill after attending a meeting of Baltimore merchants, and pneumonia developing, he had passed away at the age of 70. In his 34 years in business he had made himself known all over the world. The high reputation of his house on both sides of the Atlantic was second to none. His death was regarded in Baltimore as a public calamity as there was no civic or State movement in which he did not play a prominent part. Whether politically, socially, or in the fields of commerce and finance, he was a forceful and dominant figure whose advice and influence were always at the disposal of his fellow men. The shock of their father's death on the four sons is reflected in their letters. It was naturally felt most by the three younger sons in America, for (as George put it) " the head that thought for us is gone ". Their first reaction in America was to wind up the business. All were wealthy men and (said George, in a letter to William): " Employment is more an object with us now than the mere acquisition of more wealth." Alexander Brown had made his Will in 1823, shortly before leaving on his first and only trip to England. It was found that he was one of the three or four richest men in America up to that time, but unlike the others, his great fortune of two million dollars had been derived not from speculating in real estate but from trading. He had indeed been " *a discoverer of countries and a finder out of commodities* "; and, in the words of the Elizabethan writer, Nicolas Breton, he had proved to be " *the exercise of the Exchange, the honour of credit, and the understanding of thrift . . . the pillar of a city, the enricher of a country* ". He had built up, with his sons, a great international business on a basis of integrity and fair dealing. " There was always a disposition among customers ", he once wrote to William in the early days of the Liverpool house, " to believe that we buy their goods always at the lowest price and sell them at the highest. They are, because of this belief, usually in a suspicious frame of mind. It is accordingly essential for us in all our dealings not only to be fair but never to have the appearance of unfairness." That was the inheritance that has passed from father to son, through five generations—a reputation for fairness, soundness,

LIVERPOOL IN 1810

The first dock (Princes) was being built when William Brown established himself as a merchant in Liverpool.

From a contemporary water-colour in the Liverpool City Library.

PARISH CHURCH OF ST. NICHOLAS, LIVERPOOL. (1817)
This Church and the Town Hall (the dome of which can be seen)
are all that remain from the days when William Brown settled in
Liverpool. It was at this Church that William Brown and his
family worshipped. The tower replaced the original spire which had
collapsed three years earlier.
From a contemporary water-colour in the Liverpool City Library.

and integrity.

Alexander Brown was not merely the head that thought for his sons. It applied equally to civic and State projects. For example, he it was who conceived the idea of constructing the Baltimore & Ohio Railway. It was a time when Baltimore was losing trade to other ports, one of the reasons for trade being diverted being the opening of the Erie and other canals to the West. He not merely took the initiative in raising the capital for the railroad, he also made the project his own, as the following letter to William shows:

" The people in this country have lately been turning much of their attention to the formation of Railways. We send you by this conveyance two copies of the proceedings to make a Railway from this City to the Ohio River; if this is accomplished it will resuscitate Baltimore, and from the immense advantage of local situation, will make her in a short time second to no city in the Union.

The community seem to take a great interest in it and a charter has been applied for. We wish you to send us a copy of the charter of the Liverpool & Manchester Railway Company, with such recent publications on the subject and any other useful information you may be able to obtain for use relative thereto. You will see from the Pamphlet that we have Treadgold's and Gray's works on that subject already, and from Strickland's Report we have got many extracts; also Jessop's work.

The improvements that are daily taking place in the application of Steam to land Navigation make the latest improvements particularly desirable. An application will no doubt be made to Congress to permit Iron (for this purpose exclusively) to be imported free of duty, but whether it is granted or not, there can be no doubt that large quantities will be imported.

We have seen a letter to-day by a Mr. McLowsin (in the London *Pamphleteer*) which it may be desirable

D

to have. The Engineers for constructing the Manchester railway will be able to put you in the way of obtaining the best information on the subject. We may find it desirable to get a practical man out, of first rate talents. Can such be obtained, and what compensation would such a man command?"

The letter clearly shows that it was the Browns who were behind this ambitious project. Two years later, far from having waned, the interest of the Browns in the project had intensified. A letter to William was full of technical data concerning the construction work then in full swing. " Our Chief Engineer ", wrote Alexander Brown (on 12 June, 1829), " we regard as deficient in mechanical knowledge, except as he had from books. Our A. B." (himself) " and G.B." (his son George) " have had to direct the work at every point." Remembering that only the Stockton & Darlington Railway was at that time running in England, and that the Manchester & Liverpool line was not completed until 1830, it shows the enterprise of Alexander Brown. It was in that same year that he was writing to Wm. & Jas. Brown & Co., through whom the B. & O. railway had got its new Chief Engineer—a Mr. Knight—telling William that the first 13 miles of the railroad was in operation. He was, without doubt, " the head that thought " for the whole vast project. All the same, he was at times a difficult man, and clashes between the father and his eldest son William were frequent, since both were dominant, forthright men of ideas and rugged independence. George and his two brothers, John (in Philadelphia) and James (in New York) were in a different mould, and although George, being on the spot in Baltimore, was the natural choice as technical head of the house when Alexander Brown died, the new regime was William's opportunity to use his initiative and assert his independence.

They had reached the age of the specialist. Already they were evolving from Merchant Venturers to Merchant Bankers, building up over the years a large banking business with substantial resources, and confining themselves more and more to the granting of credits to merchants and to the buying and selling of foreign exchange. George was all for ending their trading adventures, feeling that shipping had become a business in itself and that their heavy dealings in cotton and tobacco, the very basis (with imports of linen) of their business up to that time, were beyond their capacity now that the directing genius had gone. But William would hear nothing of this. Although never physically strong, he was his father all over again, a trader in the old tradition, the " Heir of Adventure ". New and faster ships were built, some with a tonnage double that of the old *Armata*. George and his brothers in America had counselled a policy of curtailment; William, however, was all for expansion. The ultra-cautious George was for retrenchment—a policy of " What we have, we hold ". He would have been content to retire altogether from business. As he said to William in one of his letters:

" I am aware that some risk must be run in any business, but as our dear father used to say, that as we have now made our independent fortunes, they will increase rapidly with the accumulation of interest."

William had his way. How right he was is reflected in the balance-sheets for the following years; and even though there were rocks ahead, as will presently be seen, the house went on from strength to strength.

CHAPTER FIVE

JOSEPH SHIPLEY AND THE PANIC OF 1837

THE choice of Joseph Shipley as the man to assist
William Brown in Liverpool was largely dictated by
events in America. The opening of the New York office,
and the increasing business being done through the
Philadelphia branch, made it necessary for William to
have the help of someone closely identified with trading
conditions in that country, and particularly as Alex.
Brown & Sons no longer had the field to themselves, and
Wm. & Jas. Brown & Co. were by no means the only
important American house in England. Already,
following the French Wars, many Continental traders,
each a specialist in his particular trade and country, had
opened branches in London that were to become the
central offices of their respective houses. In addition to
the Wars, the collapse of the centuries-old Bank of
Amsterdam was yet another factor that helped London
to establish itself as the commercial and financial centre
of the world. Like Browns, these Continental merchants
were also evolving as merchant-bankers, and among them
were some, like the Barings, the Rothschilds, and Huth &
Co., who were attracted by the United States, with its
great potential, and who competed with the Browns for
a share of that business. There were others, in a different
category, who were also to be formidable competitors of
the Browns: Thomas Wilson & Co., George Wilder &
Co., and Timothy Wiggin & Co., known as "the three
W's". There was also a Baltimore merchant named
George Peabody, who was later to found George Peabody
& Co. and join forces with J. S. Morgan, and was to

36

prove in the hour of need one of William Brown's staunchest friends. Peabody had made a humble start in the London money market, his first venture in London being concerned with the purchase of steel rails for the new American railways. Morrison, Cryder & Co., and Lizardi & Co. were others in the ranks of Anglo-American merchant-bankers in the years that followed.

It was of vital importance therefore to the Browns that William's new helpmate should thoroughly understand the American market. Joseph Shipley was already in Liverpool as Agent for John Welsh, a well-known Philadelphia merchant, with full powers of attorney to act for him in Great Britain. He was a bachelor and a Quaker, belonging to one of the old families that had settled at Wilmington, Delaware, and he had come over from the United States six years previously. Under the firm name of Joseph Shipley Jr. & Company, he was responsible for all Mr. Welsh's cargoes that reached Liverpool. (Later, in 1822, the firm was known as Shipley, Welsh & Company.) He quickly gained the reputation of being a good merchant and one with a very extensive knowledge of American trade, and this reputation had not passed unnoticed either by William Brown or his father. It was a time when William's principal assistants in business were two senior clerks named Frodsham and Priestman, the former being made a limited or non-participating partner. It was in a similar capacity that Joseph Shipley was first offered an engagement. He at once consulted with John Welsh and matters were arranged to the satisfaction of all concerned, Joseph Shipley becoming a partner with William Brown, with Wm. & Jas. Brown & Co. taking over and conducting (through Joseph Shipley, as before) the business of Shipley, Welsh & Co. Ten years later, William E. Bowen, who for many years had represented the American house in Manchester (an appointment that first led to considerable friction between the Liverpool and American houses), was brought in as assistant to

Joseph Shipley and for a few years was also a partner in the Liverpool house, afterwards taking over the Philadelphia branch when John A. Brown retired.

That the firm continued, year by year, to expand, was due, not to a vast increase in their trading activities so much as to their gradual evolution as merchant-bankers. As the innovators among Anglo-American merchant-bankers, Browns had been first in the extensive utilisation of the documentary bill in financing the foreign marketing of American produce. Soon they were able to sell bills on England at the same rate in Boston and other centres as in New York, and small bills as cheaply as large ones, and as the interlocking partnerships in Baltimore, Philadelphia, New York and Liverpool, supported each other, this greatly strengthened their position. They went outside the family to strengthen still further these partnerships, being interested not so much in a man's financial status as in his character and ability. Wherever rivals had entrenched themselves, as in Boston and New Orleans, they sent the best men they could get as Agents—e.g. New York partner, Samuel Nicholson, to New Orleans, not merely forwarding cotton to Liverpool for the Browns, but financing its consignment by others; whilst to Boston, stronghold of the Barings, they sent Thomas B. Curtis, formerly agent of a competing merchant-banking house, Fletcher, Alexander & Co. Within two years of the arrival of Curtis in Boston, Browns undertook practically the whole of the foreign exchange business in that city. After the panic of 1837 it was on William's advice that William Bowen was posted to Philadelphia, where his wide experience and knowledge of the English market proved invaluable. It was a practice that paid handsomely, but rapid development in the firm's activities was not without its dangers as the Browns, with their customary caution, had always realised. It was doubtless in their minds when they made their offer to Joseph Shipley, since that particular year, 1825, was a year of crisis and depression in both countries, particularly in America with its shaky banking structure. It was severe in England also, the great banking house, Sir Peter Pole & Co., failing. Cotton at that time had dropped to 8⅘ cents—a quarter of its price in 1815, whilst the practice of English manufacturers of flooding the American market with their goods had ruined many of the newly established industrial firms in the United States. As a result, many merchants in the Southern ports (like Baltimore) had failed. As for the Browns, they had seen the trouble brewing and suffered comparatively little, having temporarily curtailed their activities to a marked degree.

Ten uneventful years had passed since Joseph Shipley had joined the Liverpool House. A new fleet of fast sailing-ships had been built by the Browns; their sphere of influence had extended, and no longer was linen the major item in exports to America. Cotton, however, was still the chief preoccupation of the Liverpool house. By 1836 the transactions of the firm had reached giant proportions and the inclusive returns for that year had reached the considerable total of £10,000,000 sterling. George Brown, never keen to continue in business after his father's death but persuaded to do so by his brothers, had arranged to retire the following year, but his plans were to be rudely shattered. By December, 1836, most of the outside interests of the Browns had been drastically reduced; shipments had been curtailed; stocks sold; and many outstanding accounts closed. The partners sensed an impending crisis but no one as yet realised how grave it was to be.

There were six factors that contributed to the 1837 crisis: First, there was the great absorption of capital in the U.S.A. over the previous twelve years, for railroad and canal construction, inventions of various kinds, and in the expansion of agriculture. Secondly, President Jackson had vetoed the Bill for the renewal of the Charter of the Bank of the United States, which was followed by the withdrawal of 8 million dollars of public deposits. This compelled the Bank to curtail its discounts, thus making money very tight. In turn it led to the formation of a large number of State banks, with all the evils of an expanded currency, reckless extension of credit, and wild speculation of every kind. A third contributory cause of the panic was that 1835 (or so it seemed at the time) was a year of great prosperity, and this induced extravagance in both personal and business expenditure. Fourthly, the Order issued by the U.S. Treasury in 1836, requiring payment for public lands in gold, had put a brake on the wild speculation in land at fictitious prices. A further reason for the panic was that short crops in the two previous years had been followed by dearer money which could only be obtained at increasing rates, until, in 1837, it was difficult to obtain any. Lastly, the great New York Fire, which had disorganised business and destroyed a vast amount of property, had proved a serious embarrassment to many houses, there being few American Fire Offices at that time able to meet in full the heavy claims that descended upon them.

In England, too, there had also been a very large absorption of capital in canals and railways, with extensive building and equipment of hundreds of factories. Following the establishment of the first Joint Stock bank, in 1825, no fewer than 102 were formed in ten years, and after 1835 scarcely a week passed without a new one being added to the list. Wild speculation and a reckless extension of credit followed, and in the first three months of 1836, in Manchester and Liverpool alone, 104 joint-stock companies, with a capital of over 37 million pounds, were formed for every purpose imaginable. The outflow of gold from the Bank of England began at the end of March, 1836 and continued at such a rate that an inquiry was instituted. The main causes were found to be the malpractices of many of the English joint-stock banks and the loose credit policy of several of the Anglo-American merchant-bankers. Some of these " American " houses, and many of the new banks, presented to the dealers for discount the bills drawn under the open-credit system prevalent in Anglo-American trade. The dealers used their discounted bills as collateral for loans from the Bank of England, and some of the paper discounted was so doubtful that it had certainly not been scrutinised carefully enough by receivers and buyers. The Bank of England belatedly adopted remedial measures by raising the discount rate (i.e. the bank rate), and by refusing all bills on Anglo-American merchant-bankers either as security on loans or for discount. Soon it became known that the Bank of England did not look with favour on American securities as collateral for loans or as remittances against drafts, although it was understood that no obstacle would be put in the way of discounting bills arising from " fair business transactions ". Thus a chain of events was started that caused serious embarrassment to several Anglo-American firms in February and March, and led to panic and suspension of specie payments in the United States between March and May, 1837. In England advertisements in several newspapers suddenly appeared recommending a run on the Bank of England, and these at a time when it was important that the general public should not take alarm. Prosecution of the authors was contemplated but the directors wisely decided to ignore them, and the run did not materialise. But crisis in the London money market was at hand. Remittances from the United States had slowed to a trickle by June, and many that were received could be expected to be dishonoured and returned for payment. When it became clear that many English houses would be forced to suspend payment, the Bank decided to render no more aid to discredited firms, even though guarantees were offered. On 2 June the " three W's " stopped payment, followed by five others engaged in financing American trade or marketing American securities.

Meantime, in the United States, panic was even more

severe. Runs on banks and failures of banks and business houses were commonplace in New York, Boston and Philadelphia. The price of cotton was down one half. Those who held specie began to hoard it and it became virtually impossible to negotiate a loan, so high did the rate of interest leap. Some idea of the intensity of the depression may be gauged from the fact that the State of New York, for a loan not exceeding 500,000 dollars at 6 per cent., although publicly advertised, did not receive a single bid. Never in the history of the country had there been such a catastrophe, with hundreds of firms in New York failing, factories closing down everywhere, and unemployment on a scale that was unprecedented. All banks by common agreement suspended specie payment, and credit ceased to exist. The extent and violence of the crash was something that not even the Browns had contemplated. It was by no means a critical situation for the Browns in Baltimore, Philadelphia and New York, under pressure though they may have been. They were well able to take care of themselves. But once the sensitive machinery of credit was dislocated on either side of the Atlantic, the Liverpool house was in grave peril. Panic in the United States made it impossible for the most solvent firms in England to receive their remittances. The comparatively slow sailing-ship was the only means of communication and it was a year when ships were frequently held up by unfavourable weather, with consequent delays in the arrival of cargoes on which the Browns had a lien and of the remittances and securities that would help the Liverpool house stave off disaster.

Many letters that passed between the brothers have survived, also communications that passed between William Brown and his partners, Joseph Shipley and William E. Bowen. They reveal how, by the default of others and in spite of being absolutely sound, with ample capital and surplus, they were placed in the desperate extremity of appealing to the Bank of England to support them. That the Bank did so, and to the extent of nearly two million pounds, at a time when it was denying assistance to scores of other banking houses, was a rare tribute to the integrity of the Browns who, within six months, having received the overdue funds from America, had repaid the loan, met all their engagements and a year later emerged stronger than ever. Seldom have such momentous interests depended upon the existence of a commercial firm as those which were involved in the prosperity or downfall of Wm. & Jas. Brown & Co. The ramifications of their business stretched as far north as Inverness; across to Northern Ireland; to the mills and factories of Lancashire and Yorkshire, and to the Sheffield steel-works and the Birmingham foundries. Their failure would have jeopardised the very existence of hundreds of firms and caused untold suffering and poverty to many thousands of families. How the Bank of England came to the aid of Wm. & Jas. Brown & Co. at that critical time is a dramatic story.

To tell this story it is necessary to go back to the days when William Brown first arrived in Liverpool from Baltimore in 1810. They were the days of the private banker and the choice of such was no easy matter for a stranger to decide. Much depended, for instance, on the banker's London agents, apart from their own status locally, since the failure of the London house could bring down with it as many as forty or more country bankers. For a while William had his account with the newly formed Liverpool bank of Moss & Co.

The year 1810 was one of crisis in England, and it was said that half the traders in the kingdom were bankrupt. The loss of confidence and consequent panic had arisen mainly through speculative dealings with the South American possessions of Spain and Portugal, which had been thrown open to direct trade with England. Vast amounts of English manufactures, often quite unsuitable for those countries, had been sent abroad, and had caused an inflation of prices in England. Although not so serious as the crisis of 1793, when the Liverpool Corporation actually printed its own notes to carry its traders through, it had ruined many traders and more than one local banker. When the crisis passed, the ship-owner, John Moss, had seized the opportunity of establishing the banking house of Moss, Dales & Rogers, or Moss & Co. as it was generally called, which proved to be second only to Heywoods in local importance.

William Brown appears to have transferred his account, in a short while, to Leyland & Bullins. Thomas Leyland, like Moss, was a shipowner engaged in the Africa trade. He was Liverpool's leading merchant and mayor at that time. Apparently William Brown unwittingly joined him in one enterprise concerned with the slave trade—a very lucrative venture—but when realising too late the nature of the " adventure " he promptly withdrew his account. Thereafter, his account was with the long-established Arthur Heywood, Sons & Co. which had survived the crises of 1793 and 1810. Wm. & Jas. Brown remained faithful to Heywoods. It was at the time of the 1837 crisis that the Browns came to owe their bankers a great debt of gratitude, for it was largely due to the faith and the wise counsel of John Heywood that they were supported at that critical time. Heywood's banking house, last and greatest of Liverpool's private bankers, continued until 1883, when it was bought by the Bank of Liverpool—now incorporated in Martins Bank, Ltd., the branch in Liverpool being still known to-day as Heywood's Branch. The London bankers of Wm. & Jas. Brown & Co. and agents of Heywood's bank were of the highest repute, the firm being Denison & Co. Its full title was Denison, Heywood, Kennard & Co., John Heywood being a partner. To-day, Denison & Co. is incorporated in the Westminster Bank Ltd. and (apart from an account with the Bank of England) Brown Shipley's bank accounts are still with Martins and the Westminster, a happy association that now covers a century and a half.

Towards the end of May, 1837, at a time when William Brown was ill and unable to make the journey himself, Joseph Shipley went to London to discuss the position with Denison & Co., taking with him, from William Brown, a detailed statement of the capital of the combined American and Liverpool firms and the balance sheet to 31 December, 1836, together with a list of assets and liabilities as far as could be ascertained at that date, viz., 27 May, 1837. The intention of the Browns was to pledge securities with their bankers sufficient to enable the firm to carry through without further assistance; but meantime the packet *Roscoe* had reached Liverpool on 29 May with news from the United States so grave that all hope of such an arrangement had to be abandoned, and in fact William Brown took such a gloomy view of the situation that he actually drew up a notice of suspension. Needless to say, this was never posted! His fears for the solvency of the firm turned largely on the question of the suspension of specie payments in America. He had every confidence that the three houses in the United States would be able to go on, provided the banks were able to continue specie payments. (As a matter of fact, the suspension of specie payments did not, as William Brown was convinced, embarrass the American houses. It had the opposite effect. Before that time all business transactions were at a standstill, but after the suspension, payments were resumed, and although the currency was depreciated the wheels of commerce began to turn again, and from that time there was a gradual improvement in the United States.) John Heywood and his London agents, Denison, Heywood, Kennard & Co., had at no time any doubt of the solvency of Wm. & Jas. Brown & Co. and strongly urged that the following letter should be sent to the Governor of the Bank of England:

London. 1 June, 1837.

To the Governor and Bank of England:

" After receiving the most liberal remittances from

the United States, we cannot think they would be continued to an amount equal to our wants. We find them suddenly cut off by the disastrous state of things existing there. Up to the arrival of the last packet, we had every reason to believe that we should have been able to meet our engagements regularly, without any assistance (other) than our own bankers are disposed to extend to us, but the intelligence received yesterday shows that remittances will be delayed and cut off to such an extent as to forbid the hope of our being sustained unless through your assistance.

We enclose a statement showing that our capital was about £1,350,000 at the end of this last year, and that our total engagements amount to about £1,372,000. Our losses cannot, of course, be stated, but as our debtors are among the best houses in America, and having partners, experienced in business, residing in the three principal cities where our business has been, and who hold securities for a large amount of the debts, it is quite impossible that the Bank can incur any risk in carrying us through. Were it not for the disappointment we have experienced in protested bills of exchange to the amount of £472,000, this application would not have been necessary at this time, nor perhaps at all. Of these bills, many of which are endorsed by banks, a considerable amount will be paid in part or in whole in this country. About £850 (thousand) has been sent to the United States, and the remainder is in this country, a large proportion due in the present month. Besides the disappointment of these protested bills, we are apprehensive we may also be disappointed in receiving about £370,000 which we had every reason to expect in all the present month, but which, from the disastrous accounts of yesterday, we do not dare rely upon so early.

We are, therefore, under the painful necessity of applying to the Bank for the assistance we need, and which may amount to the two above-named sums, together about £800,000, although we trust that a much less sum will be found sufficient. It will be evident from the enclosed statements that we shall, in the worst event, have a very large capital left, and we are ready to make any arrangement you propose. Besides this, our bankers, Messrs. Denison & Co., are willing to commence a guarantee list by putting down their name for £50,000 which, considering the engagements they are already under, is as much as we can expect. If time is allowed, we can no doubt obtain additions to it: and we have cotton at Liverpool and on the way of the value of about £150,000 which we would, as soon as in our power, assign over to you.

We regret the necessity of pressing this upon your attention at this moment, but as our payments must be met tomorrow, without your aid we have no alternative, and so beg to refer you to the enclosed letter from our Mr. Brown who is prevented from coming to London by indisposition, and as you will therein see, that about two-thirds of all our engagements arise out of the exports of British manufacturers, you can readily judge what disastrous consequences would follow our stoppage at this time, and which we painfully apprehend would be more felt than that of any other house in England; and as no doubt a very large proportion of our acceptances is held by the Bank, we hope you will feel an interest and find an advantage in supporting us.

Yours very truly,

(signed) W. & J. Brown & Company."

The Bank of England, it will be remembered, was at the time refusing help to many Anglo-American houses, large and small, that were in difficulties, but the case of W. & J. Brown was a very different matter. With the full facts before them they fully realised that the fall of such a house would have shaken our national credit, and so, with many expressions of good-will from the Governor and his Deputy, the Bank agreed to advance (on protested bills satisfactory to the Bank) a sum sufficient to provide for the firm's needs until the next meeting of the Court of Governors in a week's time. Writing at once to William Brown, Joseph Shipley tells him of the respite they had been granted:

" The Bank views our position as altogether different from most of the others, as it really is, and when the Board adjourned last night, they authorised the Governor to loan us, as he is doing, upon the protested bills . . . They will take in the same way (at from 16 to 20 shillings on the pound) all we have, provided they are as unobjectionable as the present lot. The Governor and the Deputy Governor assured me the Bank had expressed an earnest wish to see us carried through, which they are sure can be accomplished, and that as far as they can personally do so, they will aid in urging our claims. They cannot at present do more than advance on the protested bills, guarantees, and any security we can give them. . . . They say they are perfectly satisfied that in no event can our whole property be swept away. I have told John Heywood all I know of our probable losses, and he says it would be madness to stop as long as we can pay on."

Meantime, the news from America was even blacker than before. It told of more and more failures, and of remittances confidently expected that were delayed or suspended. This meant an increase in the estimate of possible losses, and William Brown, a sick man at his home, Richmond Hill, was inclined to take an even gloomier view of the situation. If he had had his way he would have stopped payment there and then, knowing that the firm was still solvent and that it could meet every obligation in full. As a man of scrupulous honesty he shrank from the thought of running any risk that might involve his friends and clients in ultimate loss. To Joseph Shipley he wrote:

" Certainly it is our duty, if we can, not to let the public suffer by our suspending payment, but we could

LETTER OF CREDIT. (1838)

Introducing Jerome Napoleon Bonaparte, nephew of Emperor Napoleon.

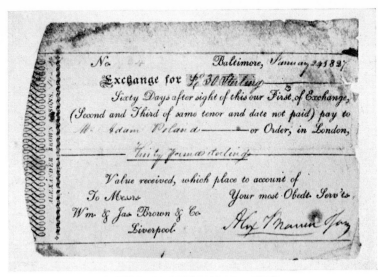

A BILL OF EXCHANGE. (1827)

Drawn by the "parent" (Alex. Brown & Sons, Baltimore) on the "son" (Wm. & Jas. Brown & Co., Liverpool).

AN EARLY DRAFT. (1835)

Drawn by Brown Brothers & Co., New York on the partner-firm in Liverpool, Wm. & Jas. Brown & Co., which, two years later, became Brown, Shipley & Co.

never forgive ourselves if we got our bankers and other friends to commit themselves largely and then were obliged to stop."

Next day came news of the failure of the three Anglo-American houses, " the three W's ". This made doubly difficult the task of William E. Bowen who was visiting Manchester, Birmingham and other centres in turn in order to secure additional guarantees. It was at least a chance for William Brown to discover who were his true friends! Came 8 June, and again the Bank gave assurances that Browns' payments would be taken care of until the next meeting of the Court, security as before to be provided either in protested bills satisfactory to the Bank, cotton on hand or to arrive, and a promise of securities to be pledged both in England and in the United States (those in America being lodged with the Second Bank of the United States), together with a guarantee list of at least £400,000 in a form suitable to the Bank of England. With this good news, Joseph Shipley left for Liverpool, and there was great excitement when it became known.

On 13 June Joseph Shipley was back once more in London with fresh facts and figures to lay before his bankers, Denison, Heywood, Kennard & Co. and, later, before the Governor of the Bank of England. He was able to show that, after everything was done, the Browns could not fail to have a surplus of two million dollars. The Bank agreed, by unanimous vote, to see the firm through to the end of the year. Thus the total amount which the Bank of England came under obligation to advance to the firm was no less than £1,950,000. Of this amount, £1,100,000 was to cover their liabilities for acceptances and book debts, the remaining £850,000 for other liabilities on endorsements. These were, of course, the obligations of the Liverpool house alone; the Bank did not and indeed could not become responsible for any of the obligations of the three American houses which, in any event, were well able to

E

take care of themselves. The grant of so large a sum—close on £2,000,000—to a private firm was without parallel in commercial history, not only in England but in the whole world. It was, without question, the highest testimony that could be paid to the integrity of William Brown and his colleagues.

Joseph Shipley, having heard the happy result of his labours, wrote immediately to William Brown, despatching it by the express mail-coach. "All is right with us here", he wrote, setting out the conditions that have already been referred to. When the news reached Liverpool the cotton market advanced a quarter of a penny and the whole town was elated. As William Brown said, when conveying to Joseph Shipley the relief he felt at this happy outcome: "It must be a pleasing reflection to us that, so far from bolstering a case up, we have made every allowance that we considered by possibility necessary, which, eventuate as it may in our receipts, it will be pleasant to reflect on." By November the firm's position had considerably improved, and Joseph Shipley, writing from London, says: "The Governor (of the Bank of England) told me . . . there was great satisfaction at the state of the account." Before the end of the year—only six months after the Bank had come to their aid so promptly and generously—the firm had repaid all the money advanced, having meantime received funds from their American houses more than sufficient to enable them to meet all their engagements in this country. Thus was averted a great commercial catastrophe that would have brought ruin to the Lancashire Cotton trade in particular and also to a vast number of manufacturers throughout the country. The Bank of England, through their solicitor, afterwards complimented W. & J. Brown & Co. by saying that the Bank had never had a more satisfactory transaction with any house.

The happy ending to this exciting story of the crisis was the endorsement, by the three brothers, of William Brown's recommendation that, in recognition of the part played by Joseph Shipley, he should henceforth be made a participating partner in all four houses and that his name should be perpetuated by changing the name of the English firm to Brown, Shipley & Co.

CHAPTER SIX

NEW PARTNERS IN BROWN, SHIPLEY & CO.
MAKE THEIR MARK

WHEN the crisis was over it was rumoured in the
United States that the Browns had lost heavily,
particularly in Cotton. In fact, their losses in America
were substantial but not too serious, and in Liverpool
infinitesimal—a mere £17,000 as far as Brown, Shipley
& Co. were concerned. This was an amazingly low figure,
considering that, only a few months earlier, nearly two
million had been needed to carry them through. On
18 January, 1838, George writes from Baltimore to his
brother William:

"... We have no difficulty in selling our bills
anywhere ... Our credit is just as high as it ever was,
and there are no regular bill sellers except ourselves in
this place ... indeed we are pressed to sell more than
we are desirous of, so that if James (in New York)
finds them heavy, we can increase our sales."

Later, on 30 March that year, he is writing to his brother
James:

" The annual accounts are received ... The winding
up of the year's business is really surprising on both
sides (of the Atlantic) and almost leads one to believe
there is some mistake, or that the estimate of losses is
not sufficiently large. However, be that as it may, I
hope by the end of the present year we will have made
up all our losses and stand as well as we did
31 Dec. 1836."

These hopes were more than fulfilled—to the great
surprise of the rumour-mongers and the satisfaction of

the partners. Although continuing to forward to Liverpool and receive consignments, as well as to buy and sell on their own account, the Browns devoted far more of their capital than before to the purely financial side of facilitating American trade. This was largely forced upon them by the state of affairs following the Panic. Most of the Southern Factors had either failed or were in bad credit and, as a result, buyers of cotton had despatched agents to the South. Through Samuel Nicholson, in New Orleans, Browns took the lead in implementing the letters of credit brought by these agents, many of whom were bankrupt merchants sent there by British, American and Continental buyers. Although most of these representatives were devoid of personal credit, they carried letters of credit from undoubted firms. Browns, through Nicholson and their other agents, advanced money for buying cotton, charged interest on these advances, purchased the bills issued under the letters of credit after the shipping documents for the purchased cotton had been attached to the drafts, and used them as remittances to cover bills drawn either on American firms or on British houses as advantage at the moment dictated. 75 per cent. or more of the cotton shipped from New Orleans at that time went to the Liverpool and Continental markets under Browns' system. In one shipping season over 200,000 dollars was made through Nicholson's agency alone, and Browns were the leading buyers and sellers of bills in New Orleans.

It was the same story in Boston, where Thomas Curtis had the agency. Virtually the whole of the foreign exchange business in that city was done through the Browns. The addition of new techniques to their practice in advancing the full market value on exports to selected correspondents, and of encouraging clients to use uncovered credits on other British merchant-bankers, enabled the Browns to meet successfully the intense competition with which they were faced when Baring

Brothers, Rothschilds and others entered the field. It was a practice that ensured a steady flow of cotton to Brown, Shipley & Co. in Liverpool for sales on commission. It also brought to Browns, through Curtis, some of the strongest houses as correspondents. The charge was $\frac{1}{2}$ to 1 per cent. for the advances, upon which 6 per cent. interest was charged. The rate of exchange on all documentary bills was usually fixed at 1 to 3 per cent. below the posted rate for A1 clean bills. Other financial houses usually left the rate to be fixed on the date that the bill was drawn, when a decline on the rate was rigged. It was not only the cotton and tobacco trades but also the immense Rio coffee business that was at that time financed by the Browns, and it was said that this trade, originating in Boston and elsewhere and remitted for in Boston, was through Curtis's agency and that this business alone called for £500,000 Sterling of bills yearly. It is clear from the correspondence that William Brown had more than a small share in dictating the policy of the American houses, and the four brothers continued the same practice of consulting with each other on all matters of major importance, and worked as a closely knit team. The losses of one house were shared by the others, and each brother took his equable share of the profits as a whole.

The Browns handled vast quantities of cotton for the Lancashire mills and one of their ships, the *William Brown,* is shown (facing page 60) drying and repairing sail and loading cargo for the Liverpool market. The scene is the spacious timber quay at New Orleans in 1834, with its massive timber bollards and its make-shift " office " under a tarpaulin. The ship, by this time, was about ten years old and in the late 1820's held the record for the fastest crossing to Liverpool. The hull gives a clear idea of the battering-ram bluff bows of this old Western Ocean " wagon ".

In Liverpool, a young man who was to play a leading part in the fortunes of Brown, Shipley & Co. was already making his mark as assistant to Joseph Shipley. This was F. A. Hamilton. It was the practice of the firm, as with most prominent merchants, to apprentice youths by articles of indenture, usually for seven years. Their training completed, they would then go off for further experience elsewhere, often returning to take up executive duties with the original firm. Young Hamilton, having finished his training, was offered business by two Manchester firms in Savannah and as his interests were primarily in cotton was inclined to accept. It was a time when George Cumming was Brown Shipley's agent in Savannah, and apparently the Exchange business there had dropped to nil. It was typical of the self-confidence of Hamilton that when William Brown asked him if he could explain the cause, and if he could bring more life into it, he replied that he felt pretty sure he could do so, stating clearly his reasons. William Brown promptly wrote to his brother James and, in due course, Hamilton was offered the agency of the firm. Before accepting, he first joined the staff of William Stuart in Liverpool in order to learn all he could about Sea Island cotton. Eventually he went, not to Savannah as originally planned, but to New Orleans as agent. This was in 1839, and during the six years he was there, there was not a single loss, and Browns' Exchange business increased enormously. At first the Exchange business was in clean bills at that port, before the Bills of Lading system came into existence. So successful was he that, in 1845, James Brown wrote him, offering him a partnership if he would return to Liverpool. It was a time when William Brown was contemplating standing for Parliament, and Joseph Shipley's health was bad and he was looking forward to returning home. F. A. Hamilton accepted, and two years later, to help deal with the increased business of Brown, Shipley & Co. they were joined by George Alexander Brown who (like his brother Stewart Brown of the New York Office) had been trained in the Baltimore house of Alex. Brown & Sons. It was not George Brown's first visit to England; he had had the distinction of riding with Stevenson on the first engine to make the trial run on the Liverpool-Manchester railway, and was also present (as an invited guest) the following year, 1831, when the railway was officially opened, and when one of their number, Mr. Huskisson (Member of Parliament for Liverpool, and a former Cabinet Minister), who had alighted from the carriage on to the track, was killed by a shunting engine. George A. Brown had a good deal of his grandfather in him; as for instance his love of ships and the sea. With a friend he once chartered a schooner and loaded it with goods likely to sell in Mexico, being chased by pirates for several days before eventually escaping. He had next been a stockbroker for some years before finally joining Brown, Shipley & Co. When William Brown was elected, in 1846, as Member for what was then the South Lancashire Division, the management of Brown Shipley was left almost entirely in the hands of Joseph Shipley and F. A. Hamilton, who were to become, in the years that followed, the closest friends. It was a friendship that was to be severely tested at the outbreak of the Civil War, when British interests favoured the Southern cause and the American partners were equally convinced of the justice of the Northern cause.

In 1850 the continued ill-health of Joseph Shipley necessitated his retirement and he left for his home at Wilmington, Delaware. Securing a replacement of his calibre was, on the face of it, well-nigh impossible, but Brown, Shipley & Co. were particularly fortunate in their selection of Mark Wilks Collet to take his place. His early experience and the story of how he came to join Brown, Shipley & Co. is told by him in the following letter:

"I was taken to Liverpool in June 1832 by Mr. Henry Patry, to learn business in his house, Henry Patry & Co., a branch of Thomas Wilson & Co., London, whose name was adopted for the Liverpool

branch a year or two later, when it become Thomas
Wilson & Co.; although a distinct partnership, Mr.
Patry being partner only in the Liverpool firm; so
that when, in the great crisis of 1837, the three great
American houses in London—Thomas Wilson & Co.,
Geo. Wilder & Co., and Timothy Wiggin & Co., the
' 3 W's '—went down, the Liverpool house of Thomas
Wilson & Co. remained solvent and liquidated. The
firm of Purton, Parker & Co. was formed to take up
the business. I continued with them as a clerk, but
they were not successful, and it was, I think, in 1840
that I accompanied Mr. Purton to the United States
to try to recover some of the reclamations on cotton
consignments that were due to the firm in Georgia and
New Orleans, but with so little result that after a
second fruitless winter spent in the U.S., I urged
Mr. Purton to give up the House and turn to something
else. His old friend, Mr. Joshua Bates, offered him a
position, which was afterwards made a partnership,
in his Liverpool firm of Baring Brothers & Co., which
he held until his death not many years after. I was left
stranded in my mercantile career, but was offered the
post of sub-manager of the Bank of Liverpool, which
I accepted and held until 1848 (making valuable
friends and gaining useful knowledge and experience),
when Mr. J. W. Cater offered me to be his partner in
London, where we carried on a West India business,
which led to my visiting the West India Islands for
two consecutive winters, returning by way of New
York. It was, I suppose, in 1849 that Mr. Cater took
over the New York firm of Aymar & Company, which
Mr. Gaillard and myself conducted until 1851, when I
joined B. S. & Co. in Liverpool."
Once again Brown, Shipley & Co. had made the right
choice, for not only had they secured the services of a
man experienced in both commercial and financial
matters, but one who knew such matters both from the
American and English angle. He was, too, a very fine

linguist, particularly French, Russian and German, and it was said more than once of him that he was one of the best-informed men on commercial and banking matters in the City of London. (As will presently be seen, he was to become Governor of the Bank of England from 1885 to 1887.) No man was better qualified to take the place of Joseph Shipley than Mark Collet who dovetailed perfectly with F. A. Hamilton. The latter had the reputation of being one of the greatest experts on cotton and he was frequently called in to settle local disputes when the quality of cotton was challenged as not being up to sample. The former, in addition to a wide experience of merchanting, had the financial experience that enabled him to concentrate on credits and financial business generally. The Liverpool house was, of course, still largely engaged in handling vast quantities of cotton on consignment, and of manufactured exports for forwarding. They had their own large warehouses and warehousing staff and their own ships. Their activities were of the most varied character and their business constantly increasing; what was remarkable was how the partners contrived to deal with their many-sided activities and to devote so much attention not only to detail but to correspondence. Many of their letters must have taken an hour or more to write, and as hand-written letters were the only means of communication in those days, they were an essential part of their daily routine. Some of the letters are highly amusing, particularly those concerned with their fleet. This letter from William Brown referring to the Captain of their ship *Sally* is typical:

"We are extremely sorry and concerned to advise you that Captain Howlan has conducted himself in such a manner since his arrival that he is totally unfit to be trusted with command of the ship. From what we learn he had been in a state of intoxication since his arrival. He seldom went near the ship, and when he did it was to fight with the mate. Yesterday Howlan got so drunk that he opened a cask of rum on board and distributed to all hands in tumblerfulls, and prevented the flour from getting on board. Howlan went ashore at a late hour and spent the night at the watch house. We have taken the necessary (step) of discharging the Captain and hope you will approve this measure, and have got Captain McKown to promise to take charge of the ship."

The Browns' ships were all American built, and were faster and bigger than the old *Armata*. The registered owners were shown either as George Brown, or as George Brown et. al., of Baltimore. Most appear to have been double-decked three-masted ships with a tonnage of 500-800 tons. As was the custom, many of them were named after members of the family, the ladies being particularly honoured. For instance, there was the *Grace Brown*, built in Baltimore in 1832, and named after the wife of the founder of the firm; and the *Isabella* (1841), named after the wife of George Brown. The *Leila*, however, appears to have been named (1838) after the heroine of Bulwer-Lytton's popular novel of the day— "Leila, or the Siege of Granada". One can understand the choice of *Hibernia* as a name for one of their ships; also the naming of another one *Tobacco Plant*—a reminder that much of the tobacco at that time was being carried (for Copes of Liverpool) in Browns' ships. Other ships were the *William Brown* (which in 1827 made the fastest time for the crossing from New Orleans to Liverpool up to that time, viz. 26 days) and the *Alexander*.

An interesting letter, dated 12 April, 1848, gives the pay and allowances of a Ship's Captain. Addressed to Capt. Benson, it reads as follows:

"As you are about to proceed to New York to take command of the Ship *Leila*, we now state your terms which are as follows: Fifty dollars a month wages. Five per cent. primage on all freight other than owner's property. Five per cent. on all steerage passengers, being considered the same as freight. One hundred dollars for cabin stores from all ports north of Savannah, and thence to Europe and back, and one hundred and fifty dollars from all ports south of Savannah. Your board to be paid in all foreign ports. Our friends in the different Southern Ports are James A. Adger & Company, Charleston; George E. Cummings, Savannah; Morrell Dickey, Mobile; Samuel Cassin, Apalachicola and Samuel Nicholson of New Orleans, on whom you will of course call on your arrival at either of these places. With our best wishes for your success."

Writing in 1909, after being a partner for 45 years, John Crosby Brown has given a vivid account of Brown, Shipley & Co. and how it operated a century ago. Cotton was usually bought and sold on the open square behind the Liverpool Town Hall, still known as Exchange Flags. The old Cotton Exchange was to the side of the Town Hall, and the stone-flagged square was surrounded by a colonnade under which, in bad weather, the cotton brokers and merchants did business. Payments were in gold, Bank of England notes, or short sight drafts on London. The only cheques drawn in the office of Brown, Shipley & Co. were on the Bank of England, usually one each morning, to meet the day's requirements of the cashier. At the end of the day all notes and gold were deposited in the Bank of England (which had its Liverpool branch nearby) apart from a small amount which might be needed after banking hours. " On a busy day, when transactions on the Cotton Exchange were large ", John Crosby Brown writes, " I have seen a long row of boys from brokers' offices, with bags of gold on their shoulders and Bank of England notes in their pocket-books, waiting to make their settlements with our cashier." At that time it was the practice of banks in Liverpool to charge a commission of one-quarter per cent. on all accounts subject to check—a practice that continued long after it had been modified or abandoned

THE " WILLIAM BROWN " AT NEW ORLEANS, 1834

From the oil-painting by Gordon Ellis

in London. In the cashier's department at Brown, Shipley & Co. several clerks were necessary on a busy day to weigh or count the sovereigns, enter all Bank of England Notes by number, and check the interest calculations on short sight drafts, in order to avoid payment of commission to the bank. Each transaction was first entered in a day-book, then into a journal, from which it was again posted into the ledgers. Among the latter was a series known as " Account Current Ledgers ", and into these all transactions were posted in full from day to day. A transcript of these ledger records, in turn, became the merchants' account current, rendered half-yearly. Every entry for the preceding six months had to be called over six times before errors could be corrected and a true balance obtained. It was a wasteful practice and it was often six weeks before the ledgers could be balanced, and irate clients in the Southern States, clamouring for permission to draw on their balances, were frequently annoyed at the delay. Modern methods both of book-keeping and office work generally had not, at that time, been evolved, but the office of a Liverpool merchant was considered a fine training ground for any youth embarking on a Mercantile career, none being more sought after than Brown, Shipley & Co.

Following the 1837 crisis and the retirement of George Brown in Baltimore in 1839, the business of the firm and its policy were controlled by William, in Liverpool, James, in New York and John A. Brown in Philadelphia. The dry-goods business on the American side had been severely curtailed as the foreign exchange and international credit business of the firm became so important; but even when the steamship began to compete with the sailing-ship the Browns, always merchant venturers at heart, were reluctant to give up their shipping interests. For a few years they remained unconvinced that the sailing-ship would be ousted, even when, in 1840, the Cunard steamship, *Britannia*, carrying the regular mail between the United Kingdom and the United States, and sailing from Liverpool to Boston, carried up to 115 passengers and averaged 14 days for the run. William, and his brother James, could remember occasions, admittedly very rare, when one of their own sailing ships had made the voyage to Cape Clear, off the south coast of Ireland, in 11 days; but they conveniently omitted to mention that, the ship meeting with a headwind, it took a further six days to beat up the Channel to Liverpool!

The *Britannia* was a wooden steamer of 1,154 tons, 207 ft. in length, with engines developing 740 h.p. It is interesting to note that, in 1844, she became ice-bound in the port of Boston—the first and only time such weather conditions have been known there. She was able to get away to schedule through the public spiritedness of the Boston merchants at whose expense a seven-mile channel was cut through the ice. The Cunard Line, with its Government subsidy, developed rapidly, and when it was realised that the famous Yankee clippers were losing the freight trade to the Cunard steamships, Congress at length agreed to support an American steamship line that would carry the American mails to Britain, and James Brown and his brother William supported E. K. Collins, a public-spirited New York merchant, in establishing the Collins Line. Their first steamships, the *Arctic,* the *Atlantic,* the *Baltic* and the *Pacific* were bigger than those of Cunard, being capable of carrying 2,000 tons of cargo and from 200 to 300 passengers. When their first ship—consigned to Brown, Shipley & Co. in Liverpool—reached the Mersey, it aroused a great deal of interest among the seafaring fraternity and no little derision, on account of its appearance, as it was the first to be built without any bowsprit or over-arching stem. That the same principle was afterwards adopted in all modern steamships is an indication of the skill and high standard of American naval architects at that time. The Collins Line was the first to provide a barber's shop, a ladies' cabin, baths, and other amenities for passengers. That his interest in the Collins Line caused no ill-feeling between William Brown and the directors of the Cunard Line is clearly shown by the close friendship that existed between them, and when a Cunard ship was seized by the United States, following an accusation of smuggling, the bond of £30,000 which was demanded, and which had to be put up by a citizen of the United States, was furnished at the request of William Brown by Brown Brothers & Co., New York. For many years after this incident a partner of Brown Brothers & Co. acted as bondsman for the Cunard Steamship Co.

These American ships each had three masts and a generous spread of canvas to aid the engines when winds were favourable. Built of oak, like the battleships of the period, the Government made it clear that, if necessary, they might be taken over as auxiliary cruisers. Their cost was about 675,000 dollars each, and there is no doubt that the partners, whether in New York or Liverpool, were at times made conscious of the fact that they had a very considerable sum invested in the Collins Line. The letter-books of Brown, Shipley & Co. also show how big a slice of the partners' working day was taken up by shipping matters, many being of such a trivial character as to make one wonder why a partner's time should be occupied by so much detail, even though Brown, Shipley & Co. were part-owners of the line and its agents in Liverpool. For instance, James Brown had written Brown, Shipley & Co., criticising the victualling of the *Atlantic*. Apparently certain passengers had complained to the President of the steamship company in New York that they could not get onions at their meals, or fresh fruit, particularly apples; and that the oranges aboard were uneatable; the raisins musty; and the wines and spirits served either too expensive or (in the case of spirits) in short supply. Apart from food and drink, the captain had complained that there was insufficient coal put aboard. It was a time when William Brown had again been ill and had gone to Southport for a change of air, and it was F. A. Hamilton who was called on to reply to the charges, most of which were unfounded. He began by saying that the Steward had full authority to order whatever was required and only if anything was " out of season or exorbitant " was it questioned. " The onions are complained of as being too large for cooking ", writes Hamilton, " they are the long Portugal onions, and the order was sent for this description. With respect to the apples, we have no eating apples in England (at this particular time of year) and the apples sent on board were baking apples, but about them and the green walnuts, we cannot explain why they did not keep . . . Oranges were not to be had, except of poor quality and at a very high price, and the writer called the attention of the Captain and Steward to this . . . when the invariable answer has been: ' We must have some for sick people.' With respect to wine, we have to say that we found on board the *Atlantic* (by the storekeeper's report) 1,251 bottles of wine, 364 bottles of spirits, 172 bottles of porter, and 6 gals. of cooking wine and brandy, and a large portion of this consists of wine put aboard in New York . . . We have always put aboard a *good* wine but your passengers do not seem to appreciate it, so we will in future give them cheaper ' tonic ' as you suggest . . . " As for the coal put aboard being 200 tons short of requirements: " Captain Nye merely judges that the coal was short by the space it occupies. We thought it had been determined there was to be no guess-work in such matters, but that the coal was to be regularly weighed as it was used, and the quantity put on board checked in this way. Either the Captain should attend to these matters or not to interfere with us when we would have proper people to manage it."

Victuals and coal were not the only trouble. Brown, Shipley & Co. were blamed for not making a greater effort to persuade passengers to cross to America in Collins' ships rather than in Cunarders. The suggestion was made (from New York) that as Brown, Shipley & Co.,

AN INDENTURE OF APPRENTICESHIP. (1842)

Apprenticeship with William Brown was for seven years, a boy's father undertaking to keep him suitably clothed and to pay all doctors' bills incurred during the period of apprenticeship. The youth received £5 for the 1st and 2nd years, £10 for the 3rd and 4th years ; £15 for the 5th and 6th years ; and £20 for the 7th and final year. Apprenticeship was not as a bank-clerk but " as a merchant " and, despite the meagre pay, it was considered a privilege to be apprenticed to William Brown.

S.S. " ADRIATIC ".   (1857)

The Browns had a large stake in the Collins Line which, a century
ago, competed with the Cunard Steamship Co. for the trans-Atlantic
trade.

The Collins boats were the first to be built without any bowsprit or
over-arching stem—a design later to be adopted by all shipbuilders.
The " ADRIATIC " carried 2,000 tons of cargo and 200/300 passengers. When she first arrived in Liverpool (in 1857) a partner in
Brown Shipley said of her: " She certainly is a magnificent vessel,
but there has been an awful waste of money on her."

From a contemporary oil-painting.

as agents, were not succeeding in their efforts, a man of their own choice, named Canning, should be sent over, and be paid £500 a year salary. Nowadays he might be described as a P.R.O., and he was to mix with would-be passengers in the local hotels and persuade them to travel by Collins Line rather than by Cunard. Brown, Shipley & Co. were furious at the suggestion, believing that their own clerk, in charge of the Passenger Dept., could not be bettered. They resented the suggestion that a man over whom they had no control should be foisted on them, and that Brown, Shipley & Co. should be called on to bear (what they regarded as) the "enormous salary" mentioned. As for the idea of contacting passengers beforehand and trying to persuade them to travel by a Collins' boat (says F. A. Hamilton):

"Passengers go in those boats that suit them best, so no amount of talking makes much difference with them . . . Many tell us they will never go by Cunard boats again, but we continually find them going nevertheless. We also fear that if a clerk in our office got in the habit of going to the hotels, we should have no control over him. He would very soon get into the habit of smoking cigars and drinking brandy and water with the passengers if he had not more firmness than most of them. With these views before you, we must leave you to act as you think best."

And needless to say, the Mr. Canning referred to by Mr. James Brown did not arrive in Liverpool as originally planned, neither was there any further attempt to introduce high-pressure salesmanship in Brown, Shipley & Co.

For a year or two the Collins Line (which was controlled by the United States Mail Steamship Company) whilst enjoying a Government subsidy proved fairly lucrative for the Browns, both in Liverpool and New York. Soon, however, there were serious problems to consider. The Collins' boats were paddle steamers, built of wood, and depended on an adequate subsidy in

F

order to pay their way. Cunard, on the other hand, were turning to screw-driven vessels, constructed of iron, and had not to suffer the same degree of uncertainty of knowing whether the substantial subsidy they received from the British Government would be renewed. William Brown, through F. A. Hamilton, evolved a plan under which the two Shipping Companies would jointly handle all transatlantic mail, but it came too late to have any chance of success. Then came disaster. The *Arctic,* described as " the most splendid of Atlantic steamships ", was run down by a French vessel in a fog off Newfoundland, in September, 1854. The crew seized the lifeboats and put off, leaving the passengers to perish. One of James Brown's sons and several other members of his family were on board and were drowned. Eighteen months later, another of their ships, the *Pacific,* left Liverpool for New York and was never heard of again. Despite these disasters plans were made for the building of a great new steamship, to be called the *Adriatic.* At that moment, however, Congress chose to reduce very considerably the subsidy for the mails, and, in addition, another financial crisis loomed up in both America and Britain. This, as will presently be seen, proved to be the end of the Collins Line and of Browns' interest in shipping. Their fleet was eventually sold, and in 1858 the last of the Collins' ships stopped sailing under the American flag. Undoubtedly it had cost the Browns a good deal of money, but no one can read the voluminous correspondence on the subject that passed between Liverpool and New York offices, without realising how much excitement and real interest the partners got out of this " adventure ".

CHAPTER SEVEN

THE 1857 CRISIS AND THE AMERICAN CIVIL WAR

BEFORE dealing with the 1857 Crisis, one result of which was the ending of the Browns' shipping ventures, mention must be made of the 1848 Crisis, even though Brown, Shipley & Co. and the American houses were able to take it in their stride. Conditions of trade in both countries suddenly changed in the first few months of that year. Prices were falling everywhere; American imports of dry goods and iron and steel were drastically reduced; there was revolution in France, and the failure of many French merchants in America, England, and in France itself; the Chartist riots had broken out in Britain; there was also an outbreak of cholera in Russia, which put a brake on the Baltic trade. All these and other factors were contributory causes of the sudden recession that developed. There had been vast spending on American railroad construction, and it was from Britain that the rails had to come. Owing to the low state of American credit, the London market was almost closed to U.S.A. borrowers and the cash for the iron and steel had to come from the United States itself. To attract the money, very high rates of interest on railroad issues had to be offered. In England money was tight; speculation in railways had collapsed; prices fell; and there were many failures among merchants, particularly among cotton brokers. Unemployment and labour unrest followed the falling-off in the demand overseas for manufactured goods, and there was concern over the repeal of the Corn Laws. To Brown, Shipley & Co., however, most of this dismal position had been foreseen, and with sails furled they were able to ride the storm. Not that the crisis was nearly so grave as that of 1837, or as severe as the one that was to follow nine years later in 1857.

Writing from Liverpool on 28 October, 1857, F. A. Hamilton tells his old friend and colleague, Joseph Shipley, living in retirement in Wilmington, U.S.A., how Brown, Shipley & Co. were meeting the crisis:

" Times have come upon us such as I must confess I was not prepared for, tho' I could not but think for some time past a clearance was approaching, and from this side we have accordingly again and again been urging the necessity of realising all lock-ups and getting ourselves into position to meet anything that might happen, and I flatter myself that the course pursued has not altogether been without its benefit. . . . I believe few houses are entitled to a higher position, and looking at the difficulties that now embarrass American affairs with a calm mind, I see nothing to create the alarm that seems to have pressed on Mr. James Brown and his brother, Mr. John A. Brown. The affairs of 1837 are very different from the present. Protested Bills to an enormous amount were thrown back on the Liverpool house, much accommodation paper was passing all round, whereas now I see no ground for apprehending any amount of protest paper on this side, and further, so far as we are concerned, every bill on us is against a legitimate business transaction. We hold bills receivable of an undoubted character sufficient to carry us into December. The engagements of the American firms are next to nothing. Tho' money here is worth 8 per cent. as a minimum, there is no difficulty in obtaining it, nor do I apprehend there will be a time for some time to come that such bills cannot be discounted at some price, for tho' there is undoubtedly undue speculation there appears to be no general or public undertakings of that magnitude to cause panic here. The Bank Act works admirably, and is now so well understood that notwithstanding the odium that attaches to it in many quarters, I am satisfied it has and will have a most conservative influence in preventing undue speculation. Though many of our correspondents have required accommodation, yet they have for the most part not only given ample security but struggled manfully to pay up so far as they could, and their settlements in cash have been to a large amount, and now they will in a great measure be relieved of the great pressure by the suspension of the banks throughout the country and by the arrival of gold to this country from California . . . With the credit of the House as high or higher than ever, with the crops now on the point of coming to market, speedy intercourse between the two countries, I cannot but believe we shall easily overcome our present annoyances . . . From your knowledge of me you know I am neither speculative nor over-sanguine, but I feel this is not a time to give place to undue fears and apprehensions, but to look the difficulties calmly and cheerfully in the face, and with God's help, we fear not the result . . . ''

A month later F. A. Hamilton is again writing to Joseph Shipley. The position in Britain had deteriorated; the Bank Charter Act had been suspended; two Glasgow banks had stopped payment; discounts had advanced to ten per cent., and there was general panic.

" During the whole of this we have maintained our position well and have escaped losses by protested bills wonderfully. The lock-ups from the cause being £60,000, of which we have only about £20,000 from which we can possibly sustain any ultimate loss, the balance being on the Scotch banks. We are provided up to the end of December within about £100,000. We never were so free of Bills on the Anglo-American houses, and I feel confidence in saying what I before wrote, that we shall safely weather the storm . . . and that the house will stand as high or higher than it ever did, and deeply thankful ought we to be for our preservation in the midst of so much ruin . . . I think we have seen the worst here. Engagements are decreasing on all sides, and people settling down to low prices. The profits for some time have been large, so that there has been a good deal to pull on. We are sure to have individual failures, however, from the heavy losses on produce, say, £5 per bale on cotton, £40 per bale on silk, etc., etc."

By December, 1857, the crisis had passed, leaving behind it a trail of ruin. In America, that year, the Bank of Pennsylvania had failed, and within four days, all banks in that State had suspended. Discount rate in New York had risen to 3 per cent. per month; demand for foreign bills had practically ceased, and sterling bills sold at a discount of from 1 to 10 per cent. Failures and suspensions were general throughout the country, but Browns stood firm.

Their only real embarrassment was the Collins Line in which they were deeply involved, and which called for large advances. This particular interest had been initiated by James Brown in New York, and a great deal of money was locked up in the enterprise. Both William Brown and F. A. Hamilton were shipping enthusiasts and, when considerable advances were needed, were quite prepared to ask John Heywood, their banker, to see them through. This of course, was *before* it was known that the United States Government was to reduce very considerably the subsidy for carrying the mails. Once that happened, as could have happened with the Cunard if the British Government had retracted, their ships lost money. They were also faced with the prospect of reducing their rates in order to meet the competition from the screw-driven vessels that were coming into the Atlantic service, their own ships being paddle steamers. Reading the correspondence that passed between the partners during the years when they were interested in the Collins Line, one senses that William Brown, the merchant venturer, was often in conflict with James Brown, the financier. The latter might have been persuaded to pull out before they were too deeply involved; but the former, a stubborn and, at times, a difficult man to argue with, had made up his mind to see it through. After all, it was a matter of prestige for Brown, Shipley & Co. that the Collins Line should not be allowed to fail. In a great port like Liverpool, where they numbered among their closest friends so many prominent shipowners, both he and Hamilton would not hear of defeat. All the same, if the Browns had never been involved, or had cut their shipping losses earlier, the partnership would have been saved a great deal of money. It was, however, the cut in the subsidy which eventually forced the decision to withdraw from shipping. A paragraph in the Liverpool newspapers, shortly after it had become known that the ships of the Collins Line were to be sold, reported that Russia was interested and might buy the fleet, but nothing came of this and they were sold elsewhere.

As will be seen from F. A. Hamilton's further letter to Joseph Shipley (written before the ships of the Collins Line were sold), the 1857 crisis had little effect on the fortunes of Brown, Shipley & Co., except to enhance their reputation:

" I am happy to inform you that everything in our business is going on as satisfactorily as could be hoped. Remittances are coming forward freely and the principal part that was under protest has been paid either by drawers or indorsers, so that the amount of protested paper held by us is now quite a small matter. The financial crisis appears to have passed, and though we may have individual failures, yet I do not apprehend any serious further embarrassment to trade. The position of the Bank of England is daily improving, engagements are running off, and I anticipate we shall see a much easier state of the money market after the turn of the year, and so far as I am concerned, I feel much less anxiety about business than I did before the panic began, for I never could hide from myself the dangers that appeared to me inevitable from the general expansion and apparent undue prosperity that existed. The position held by the house through the whole crisis has been so strong that any rumours that existed were only for a moment, and only sufficient to meet with contradiction from their own absurdity.

American matters seem to be mending fast. The *Adriatic* (one of the Collins boats, and the very latest to be built) arrived safely and she certainly is a magnificent vessel, but there has been an awful waste of money on her. I understand the U.S. Government have themselves broken the contract by not allowing postage money for the *Ericson* (another of the Collins boats). If this be so I am satisfied the wise course will be to throw up the contract and sell the boats for the most they will bring. They must lose money every trip they run, and at the end of the contract the boats will be much deteriorated. So long as they run there will be nothing but trouble for Mr. James Brown and loss to all concerned. The passage money must inevitably be reduced in the Spring to meet the screw boats, and it would be the best news I could hear, that Mr. James Brown had decided to run the boats no more."

It was characteristic of the interlocking partnership that, having been primarily responsible for the investment in the Collins Line, James Brown should assure his partners that he would himself bear the whole of the heavy loss. However, in losses as with profits, all partners willingly took their share of the responsibility.

Although the Browns had emerged from the 1857 crisis stronger than ever, they were to be faced, in four years' time, with one of the gravest threats to their unity—one that was to test to the limit the friendship and understanding that had characterised the Partnership since the foundation of the firm by Alexander Brown. This was the American Civil War, during which there were several occasions when war between Britain and the North (under Lincoln) seemed imminent. The Lancashire millowners and Liverpool cotton merchants and the ruling classes generally, were all for the South in the conflict. They regarded the secession of the Southern States as a movement of national self-determination, their sympathies being strongly in favour of the southern aristocratic communities. Although Lincoln had repeatedly declared that slavery had nothing to do with the issue, the British working class—the Radicals—regarded slavery as a very real issue in the Civil War and believed that constitutional government and national unity rested with the forces of Lincoln and the North. Once the war broke out, Britain's problem was whether she should recognise the Southern Confederacy. Lord John Russell and Gladstone were both strongly in favour of recognition and sympathised with the South. Palmerston was in favour of making no such move until the fighting had proved more conclusive. Fortunately for the future of Anglo-American relations—and for that of Brown, Shipley & Co.—it was decided that recognition should be withheld until the issue became clearer, and in fact it was never granted. Throughout the conflict and for many years after, the feeling was widespread in the American North that Britain had showed little understanding for the United States in this crisis. As will be seen in the letters that passed between the partners, friction centred mainly on two maritime disputes concerning the *Trent* and the *Alabama*. The *Trent* was a British ship from which two Southern envoys, named Mason and Slidell, were forcibly removed by a Northern naval officer. When the news of this reached Britain there was great public indignation, and had it not been for Prince Albert's intervention, which led to the toning down of Lord John Russell's despatch, and to Lincoln's wisdom, war between Britain and America would very probably have taken place. As for the *Alabama,* a cruiser built in Britain and supplied to the South, she was very successful in attacking the commerce of the North, before she was at length captured in June, 1864. The dispute concerning the supply of such ships to the Southern forces was settled only in 1872, by arbitration, and the payment of substantial damages by Britain. (How, in 1873, that payment was actually made by Britain is told in Chapter 10.)

The proclamation of neutrality issued by the British Government led to serious differences of opinion between the Liverpool and New York partners as to the proper course to pursue in the management of their business. At this particular time, with one exception, the partners in Liverpool were British—William Brown, F. A. Hamilton, and Mark Collet, the one American being Stewart Henry Brown. The English partners were unwilling to undertake any business which involved the violation of the terms of the neutrality declaration, as for instance, the shipment to either belligerent of articles contraband of war. On the other hand, the New York partners were strong Northern men and were anxious to facilitate the purchase of arms and munitions of war from Britain and the Continent. Undoubtedly the English partners took a much more correct attitude. Moreover, they were far more realistic in their assessment of the gravity of the crisis and its probable duration than were those in America, who at the time were confident that the war would end within a year. For Brown, Shipley & Co., F. A. Hamilton stated the case to the New York partners, in a letter dated 7 August, 1861.

" We have not touched on political matters of late, feeling how difficult it was to form even an idea of the future that could be expressed with any degree of confidence. Now, however, as you are granting some large Credits, which cannot be availed of for some considerable time, we think it but right to give our opinions for what they may be worth, in respect to the future course of our business in Credits.

We may premise by saying that Mr. Collet does not take as gloomy a view of the future as that held by Mr. S. H. Brown and the writer, and he before leaving home expressed, as we understood him, his concurrence in the course of granting Credits to first class people, considered to be at the present time responsible on their own merits.

We mention this on the ground that the opinion of all the partners should be fully known and appreciated, and we shall send a copy of this to him (i.e. Mr. Collet) that he may make any comments on the matter now under discussion.

I think the writer has before expressed to you the opinion which he has entertained from the commencement of this unfortunate separation of the Northern and Southern States, that this separation was final; that this decision to separate had been growing and increasing with an intensity of feeling for years and that no earthly power could reunite the two sections, but that the South were in earnest and would resist to the death . . . Is the North to give in? The belief of the writer is that eventually this will be the result, but it will take a long time . . .

What must be the effect of this, and who can look without much anxiety to the effects of large masses of people out of work during the coming winter, and a disastrous war entailing on thousands ruin and disappointment?

Supposing one or more defeats, who can foresee the moral effect? The blockade must be imperfect and Southern Privateers tempted by their latest successes will increase, and it may be next to impossible to cover the war risks. . . . If you are satisfied as to the power to suppress outbreaks . . . of a people . . . suffering from poverty and disappointment, and at the same time to carry out the blockade with efficiency, and bring the war to a happy termination, you will doubtless think that it is not well to stop granting to good people 'now', Credits spreading over a lengthened period; but the writer does not feel this confidence and his view would be to grant no such Credits and to do no business that does not speedily wind itself up, until we can see more clearly what is before us . . . You must not consider this as in any way wishing to interfere with your views as to the proper course of action, as these opinions may be worthless, but being entertained by the writer (F. A. Hamilton) he does not think he would be justified in not candidly stating them, but only as an individual opinion and as such to have such weight as you think it deserves."

To this letter Stewart H. Brown adds the following footnote:

" In the above remarks on the policy which we ought to adopt in our business, I quite agree, tho' I so much hope for an entire reconstruction, or rather resumption of supremacy by the Federal authorities over the whole territory that I am unwilling to concede that the task of recovery is at all a hopeless one. Still I should be glad to rest from such (Credits) business altogether for the present."

Meantime, Mark Collet, who was away at the time F. A. Hamilton had written the above letter but had been sent a copy of it, wrote to Stewart H. Brown, agreeing with the policy but indicating that he was inclined to take a rather more optimistic view of the American situation. Says Mark Collet:

" I confess that all the evidence that has reached me through various sources tends to the belief that if any anterior Union feeling did exist at the South, it has been extinguished by what all Southerners regard as the violent aggression of the North in taking up arms to enforce the Union, and if this be so, then there is an end of the only rational policy upon which (in my humble judgment) the war can be carried on with any hope of success.

Looking at the facts, that in the United States—unlike older countries with privileged classes—every interest must suffer seriously . . . it will be dangerous to provoke discontent . . . The whole Northern cotton spinning interest is dependent for its very existence (far more than in Europe) upon a supply of Southern cotton—I cannot bring myself to believe that a policy of subjugation (I am using the term technically for convenience) can stand the severe tests to which it must speedily be brought, and am inclined to believe that if, in the next few months, the North does not achieve some signal military successes, and thereby evoke the alleged latent Union sentiment . . . in the South, then there will arise in the North such discontent as will lead to some accommodation.

As regards the effect these views should have on the policy of our business, I wish to premise that I feel for myself that (however much I might differ from my partners' views) . . . the views of the most restrictive and conservative member of the house ought to prevail.

I have thought that if the North did not purpose to carry the policy of subjugation . . . we might go on granting credits for the necessaries of life to the really responsible of our customers, and even if the War were protracted, I cannot but think that coffee, tea, sugar, dress, etc., must be imported, and that some people must do the business, and that the war risk will be taken by responsible offices at some premiums. Still, my opinion only goes to the length of assenting to the limited granting of credits, if it be thought wise, but that, as before said, I should far prefer concurring in the view of the more restrictive of my partners (Hamilton) than urging my own. I must acknowledge, however, that there is one element not referred to by Mr. Hamilton which makes me increasingly inclined to the more prudent course. If the President really intends to act on the authority given him by Congress to collect the duties at the Southern ports in ships of war stationed outside, whilst the ports are in possession of the secessionists, it cannot fail to lead to conflict with European powers and may bring on a general war. Here is a danger that would touch us directly, and in view of which (if it is to be apprehended) I would prefer to have no distant engagement outstanding . . . Our partners in New York should look this matter fairly in the face, for a collision with France and England . . . would indeed render all business most hazardous, and reviewing all the circumstances, I shall be well content to see our credit business suspended for a time, unless the New York house see their way out of the difficulties Mr. Hamilton has pointed out, and those I have just averted to . . . "

For the first time in over half a century, there were serious differences of opinion as to policy—differences that brought the partnership perilously close to dissolution. Fortunately for all concerned, James Brown was in Paris at this critical period and was in close touch with the American minister to France, and with his brother William and the Liverpool house. He was therefore in a position to assess the situation and to advise his colleagues in New York of the official French and British attitudes. In August, 1861, James Brown writes to his son, John, in New York: " I enclose a letter for Brown Brothers & Company with my views. I fear from the temper of the North a servile insurrection will be the result, and if so, there is no knowing what ruin will overtake the North as well as the South, hence Brown Brothers & Co. cannot be too prudent and cautious, for in the end we may be embroiled with European powers and our property at sea have a poor chance of escape, capture and loss." A few weeks later, he is writing to Brown Brothers & Company: " The more and the further I see of the progress of this war . . . the more discouraged I feel for the future of our distressed country . . . As I have always said, the War we are now engaged in was inevitable." A few weeks later, as if in reply to the views of the English partners, who had counselled prudence and the utmost caution in the conduct of the business, James Brown writes: " There is such a thing in business as being over careful and over-suspicious of the integrity of parties with whom we are dealing; it makes the house unpopular. Better to be taken in and lose a little occasionally than to be so rigid as to make parties afraid to approach you." If any criticism could be levelled at William Brown or Brown, Shipley & Co., it was scarcely on this score that it could be justified. There was far too much optimism among the New York partners regarding the situation. All of them—and even Mr. Stewart Brown in Liverpool—thought the war would be over within the year, and that whilst some restriction of business was necessary, the English house was rather inclined to exaggerate the difficulties. F. A. Hamilton therefore decided that he would go and see for himself how far he and Mark Collet were justified in urging their opinions on the New York house, and on arrival he wrote to Mark Collet, telling him that he was pleased with the result of his business conversations concerning the various accounts, but had not, of course, been there long enough when writing to form an opinion on the various matters that had really taken him out there. He was apparently surprised to find so little excitement in New York and tells Collet that the one topic of conversation appeared to be the extravagance of the government and the corruption of public officials and war contractors. It seemed to him, he said, that the war would last just as long as the money lasted! In a later letter to Brown, Shipley & Co. he writes:

" My views on the position of this country are somewhat modified since my arrival in reference . . . to the danger from popular tumults. The fact is, so long as the war continues, occupation is found for a large portion of the population . . . at good wages in the Army. The pay of a private is 13 dollars a month and rations, which he can draw in kind or in money to the value of 12 dollars a month, so that his actual earnings are equal to 25 dollars. Not bad wages for a working man . . . My own views with respect to the duration of the war are not altered . . . Under any circumstances, I am strongly under the impression that no cotton will be exported from the South this year and I only wish I could see any probability of any going forward for several months to come, but I cannot."

It was during his stay there that the *Trent* affair (to which reference has already been made) took place, just as Mark Collet had foreseen. It aroused the utmost indignation in England and caused serious differences of opinion between the English and American houses. As the following letters from Brown, Shipley & Co. clearly show, the English partners believed that, following the *Trent* incident, war between the two countries was inevitable. Writing to Brown Brothers & Company on 27 November, 1861, Brown, Shipley & Co. say:

" The West India Mail Steamer *La Plata* has arrived at Southampton today and brings news of the American War Steamer *San Jacinto* having boarded the Mail Steamer *Trent* on her voyage from Havana to St. Thomas, and taken from her by force Messrs. Mason & Slidell, the Confederate Commissioners. This is considered a very high-handed measure, and the state of excitement here is such as we have never before witnessed. An indignation meeting has been called, and it is probable very strong speeches will be made. We cannot hide from ourselves that the most serious consequences may arise from this act of the United States Government . . . Under the circumstances it is thought desirable by Mr. James Brown (over from Paris) and ourselves (Mr. William Brown being unwell at home, we have not been able to consult him), that it is better to open no credits of

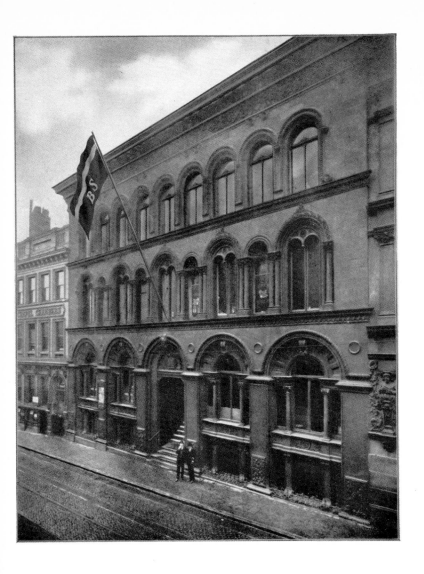

THE LIVERPOOL OFFICE OF BROWN, SHIPLEY & CO.
(1888)

William Brown's first "counting-house" was in Strand Street.
In 1814 the firm became Wm. & Jas. Brown & Co., with offices in
Union Court. In 1837 the title changed to Brown, Shipley & Co.,
the firm later transferring to larger premises in Chapel Street. The
Liverpool Office was closed in 1888, 25 years after the London
Office at Founders Court had been opened.

Chapel S.
27. April 1843.

Gentn:

We are requested by the Master of the American Ship "Rose" to inform you that Your Ship "Duke of Lancaster" came in Contact with the "Rose" last evening in the River, when the latter Vessel was riding at her Anchor, and has Caused her serious damage — and we have hereby to Notify you that the Master of the Rose holds you responsible for the said damage. —

We are Gentn

Respectfully Yours

Brown Shipley & Co

Mess.rs John Gladstone & Co
Union Court

S.S. "ROSE" IN COLLISION. (1843)

A great deal of time—and money—were expended by the Partners on their shipping interests. The "ROSE" was one of the Browns' fleet at that time. (1843)

any description until we can judge better what is to grow out of this unfortunate affair, and further, that the Havana Agency had better be suspended for the present. If you can obtain instructions from the parties on whose account we have opened credits for use in the East, for us to cancel them in case we should on receipt of your answer to this, or afterwards, see good grounds for believing in a war between our two countries, it will be well for each House to send through you to us letters to this effect to the parties using the credits. We are fully aware of the difficulty and annoyance of opening and cancelling credits and suspending contemplated agencies, but in such times when it is impossible to see what a day may bring forth, we do not see how it is to be avoided. The Funds have declined $\frac{5}{8}$ to $\frac{3}{4}$ per cent.

Since writing the above, we learn that the meeting has terminated and several parties expressed the opinion that it is not certain that the United States Government have overstepped the law . . . The share market has improved 10 per cent. from the lowest point, and Consols close a shade firmer. Opinions as to the legality of the act seem to be divided . . . With these general views we leave you to act."

Three days later, Brown, Shipley & Co. again write to Brown Brothers & Company:

" We much regret to say that political matters look even more gloomy than when we last addressed you . . . It is known that the Government have arrived at the conclusion that the boarding of the *Trent* and forcible removal of Mason and Slidell is in direct violation of all International Law, and with this view, that England has no other course left but to demand from the United States Government an ample and satisfactory apology.

We greatly fear this will not be given, and in that case we see nothing but the renewal of the horrors of war . . . Under these unfortunate circumstances, it is

G

thought by all the Partners here, that until you are satisfied that peace will be confirmed between the two countries, it will be the only safe and prudent course to suspend all credits, and to get all parties to whom credits have been granted to authorise us to cancel them.

It is also thought advisable that the Amount standing to the credit of our Mr. Collet and Mr. Hamilton in your private Books should at once be transferred to the Liverpool Books. Should War unfortunately take place, so many complications will arise that it is impossible to forsee what course will have to be adopted, and the question has been raised whether it may not become necessary to separate the English and American houses, though this is of course only an idea at present."

To emphasise the grave import of this letter from Brown, Shipley & Co. the same mail carried a letter from James Brown to his New York colleagues. It confirmed the view that war was imminent, and that the U.S. Government had unquestionably committed a breach of International Law, not in boarding a British ship—as they were entitled to do if they had reason to believe it was carrying contraband of war—but in removing the two passengers, Mason and Slidell. He advanced the somewhat novel idea that the conflict was not really a war in the accepted sense, but the suppression of rebellion in part of the Union's territory. This circumstance, James Brown claimed, had made it an infringement even to have boarded the *Trent*. He regarded it as a matter of extreme urgency that the Merchants and Bankers should take a hand in the crisis by making the strongest representation to the U.S. Government to avoid war with England, a war that "would be disastrous beyond measure to the Northern States and beyond all question throw Maryland and West Virginia into the Southern Confederacy". His view was that the Government had provoked the British Government still further by issuing a circular to the different States to put their seaboard and lake defences in order. " It seems very important that the Bankers and Merchants make themselves heard ", he went on, and after comparing the conflict with the Civil War in England in the 17th century, dealt with the treatment of British property in the United States, a question that was causing a great deal of concern in Britain. In short, both James Brown and Brown, Shipley & Co. were quite certain, by December, 1861, that war would take place. Indeed by far the strongest language regarding the confiscation of British property, whether merchandise or securities, came from James Brown himself:

" The public mind here (in England) will continue to be agitated until they can hear how our Government receives and answers the despatches gone out, and until then we can only have conjectures. If the United States could be guilty of such folly, madness, and fraud as to confiscate aliens' property in event of war, they would be no better than robbers in the eyes of the world, and I would not desire to live amongst them and call America my home . . . and desire that others should have the same feeling."

The danger of a break between the two countries, however, was happily averted. As already mentioned, this was as much due to Lincoln's good sense as to the toning down of the British despatches at the suggestion of the Prince Consort. Perhaps no single letter that passed between the partners in those fateful months shows more clearly the strained relations caused by the Civil War than that of Joseph Shipley to his old friend and colleague, F. A. Hamilton, following the final settlement of the *Trent* affair:

" I have been laid up with rheumatic gout for the last six weeks and confined to my bed most of the time . . . Your last letter found me at about the worst in body and gloomy enough in spirit, for which the political aspect of the moment gave me too good cause. The untoward affair of the *Trent* is, we must hope, finally settled, and in a way to remove I trust much of the asperity it engendered.

. . . While the diplomatic action of the British Government was all that could have been desired, the action of a great majority of the British press, and, as it appeared, of a large portion of the British people, took us by surprise.

The first impression was, I think, absolute astonishment at the degree of passionate, vindictive indignation and invective which so generally burst forth, seeing that England had herself, some hundreds of times, inflicted on our flag aggressions of the same character, but without the extenuating circumstances attending this, the first one on our part.

The House of Commons, as you know, when a new Parliament is organised, exacts from the Crown a solemn promise, that it will always put the most favourable constructions on all their words and actions. It could be wished that the spirit of this good rule could exist between nations . . . and if the news of the *Trent* had been received in England under such influence. Instead of this it seemed to be determined (I won't say exactly by common consent) to make the worst of it . . . The idea that here there was any desire for war is too absurd to waste a word upon . . . It is I think much to be regretted that the existing generation in England have so little knowledge of the political and commercial intercourse between the two countries . . . preceding the War of 1812. I can well agree with you that the capture of a thousand Rebel (i.e. Southern) envoys would be dearly bought at the cost of a rupture between our two countries . . .

As to the honour of England, of which you speak, I need hardly say to you that I would be among the last to attempt to contribute a stain upon it, and perhaps few even among her own people have felt more pride in her triumphs and prosperity than I have done, but I must confess that my feelings and sympathies have been most deeply tried during these sad last and bitter controversies."

If the American Civil War was critical for the Partnership, it had certainly proved a rare testing-ground for the close friendships that had been built up over the years between the English and American partners. It proved, too, to be the end of merchanting as far as Brown, Shipley & Co. were concerned.

CHAPTER EIGHT

THE PASSING OF SIR WILLIAM BROWN

WILLIAM BROWN'S interest in the public affairs of his adopted city began soon after his settlement in Liverpool. In 1824 he was made a Freeman of the borough, and the following year was a member of the deputation to the Government concerning the reform in the management of the Liverpool Docks, at that time exclusively in the hands of the Corporation. As a result, the Dock Board was reconstituted, 13 members being nominated by the Corporation and 8 by the ratepayers, William Brown serving for eight years as a ratepayers' representative. In 1831, he was one of the founders of the Bank of Liverpool and was its first chairman, and was Trustee of the Liverpool Fire Insurance Co. (now the Liverpool & London & Globe Insurance Co.) on its formation. In 1852 he was made Deputy Lieutenant of the County and was High Sheriff in 1863.

Throughout his life he was a consistent Free Trader and took a prominent part in the campaign for the repeal of the Corn Laws. It was on this issue that he was elected Member of Parliament for South Lancashire in 1847. It had been a time of trade depression and in the manufacturing towns there was great distress, the prices of grain and livestock being high. The poor harvest and the continued failure of the Irish potato crop made bread dear. It was in these " hungry forties " that Cobden and Bright, leading the agitation for Free Trade, laid the ideological foundations of " Victorian England " —a powerful, peaceful, and prosperous nation. Twenty-eight years after Peel's budget that had seen the repeal of the Corn Laws, British exports had increased from £47,000,000 to £200,000,000 and a period of unrivalled prosperity for the country had followed. No one was a more enthusiastic Free Trader than William Brown and he did his best to win support for his doctrine in the United States by initiating in 1850 a correspondence with the U.S. Secretary of the Treasury—a Protectionist—in the columns of the newspaper *Pennsylvanian*. The letters attracted considerable notice in prominent journals on both sides of the Atlantic. He played a leading part in the campaign for the penny post, and it is also interesting to note that he took a prominent part in the advocacy of decimal coinage and, in 1854, succeeded in the appointment of a parliamentary committee to consider the question of its adoption; but, like others since that time, he was unsuccessful in pressing for this reform.

It has been said that William Brown's influence and understanding in the field of Anglo-American relations was such that, even after he had given up his seat in the Commons, his advice was frequently sought by Cabinet Ministers. More than once that influence was exerted in the cause of peace. For instance, a boundary dispute between the two countries when Palmerston was Prime Minister had led to crisis. William Brown had facts and figures that were accessible to no one else, and feeling the responsibility of his unique position, he passed on this information to the Prime Minister. He showed how the stoppage of supplies of American cotton might result in revolution in Lancashire, and as a result of his representations there was an amicable settlement of the dispute which, had it been allowed to drag on, may well have meant war between England and America.

It was, however, during the critical days of the American Civil War that he made what was possibly his greatest contribution to peace between the two countries. The story has already been related of Britain's sympathy with the Southern Confederacy and the public outcry following the *Trent* affair. In these, his views were at variance with those of the Government of the day and with his Liverpool partners. That there was no open breach with Hamilton and Collet is a measure of their affection for him and their respect for his sincerity. He felt his position keenly and his one anxiety was to create a better understanding between the two countries. He was in constant communication with members of the British Cabinet, putting before them the real conditions in the United States as he himself knew them. He was also in touch with American Secretary of State, Seward, urging him to send to London properly accredited persons of good social standing to present the case for the North with the same degree of tact and skill as the Southern Confederacy's representatives had shown. The advice was acted upon and there is little doubt that, in stating their case, despite doing so belatedly, the heavy bias of the British public in favour of the South was in some measure counteracted. Years later, John Crosby Brown, grandson of the founder and (at that time) Senior Partner of Brown Brothers, New York, was paying a visit to Secretary Seward's son and was shown this very letter, written by his uncle. It had been filed away among the private correspondence of the Civil War period. In a further letter from F. A. Hamilton to Brown Brothers, New York, dated 19 February, 1862, there is reference to an enclosure—" a copy of a letter written by Mr. William Brown to Mr. Seward in relation to confiscation of enemy's property in time of war ". America owes much to the influence which William Brown exercised at that critical time, and to his constant efforts to preserve peace between the two countries. His efforts and those of his brother James in this connection were not always appreciated at the time and the motives behind such intervention were grossly misrepresented on occasion. Among those who tried to discredit William Brown was the *Times* correspondent in America during the Civil War, W. H. Russell—" Bull Run " Russell, as they called him in America. As a typical example of the reckless statements that were circulated, even by responsible journalists, the following letters are interesting:

The first, dated 5 January, 1863, is from William Brown to W. H. Russell:

"My attention has been called to the assertions made respecting myself and my brother in pages 4 and 5 of your 'Diary kept while in the United States' as correspondent of the *Times,* and which are so utterly unfounded that I am sure you will feel it due to yourself to publicly withdraw them.

After remarking on the subject of my nephew's visit to England, and on the birthplace of myself and my brother, both of which I may now mention are incorrectly stated, you proceed to say that 'in the War of 1812 the brothers were about sailing in a privateer fitted out to prey against the British, when accident fixed one of them in Liverpool'. Only one inference can be drawn from this paragraph, viz. that my brother and myself were on the point of engaging in privateering, which is so utterly untrue that I must request from you a public contradiction to a charge so inconsistent with the whole course of our well-known principles; for though legalised, we have ever considered it a degrading and demoralising pursuit, and there is not a member of my family who ever did or ever would embark in it, directly or indirectly, in any shape or form.

The real facts are these. I went to America for the first time in 1800, leaving my brothers at school in England. They soon after followed me to the United States, where they remained in business with my father. In 1810 I commenced in business in Liverpool, and after my marriage I proceeded to the United States, with Mrs. Brown, on a visit to my family. During the time I was there the war broke out, and we immediately returned home in the *Pacific*, the first 'cartel' (ship) after the commencement of the war.

It is my intention to wait a few days before sending a copy of this letter to the *Times*. This will afford you sufficient time to reply."

In due course the following letter from W. H. Russell was received:

" On my return to town I found your letter of 5 January, which had been forwarded to me from the *Times* Office, in which you take exception to a passage quoted from my Diary—North and South, pp. 4-5—and inform me that the statements made there are incorrect. It gives me concern to hear that I have misrepresented facts, and as there will be a new edition of my book issued shortly, I will cause your contradiction to be inserted, and the passage complained of to be omitted.

The greater part of the statement came from your nephew. The part that relates to the sailing of the privateer was told me by a gentleman on board, who said he knew your family and who further informed me that your father was implicated in the rebellion of '98 and migrated in consequence to the United States.

I need not assure anyone who knows me how sincerely I regret being made the means of spreading an erroneous story, but to you, Sir, I may add that any reparation in my power to make shall be cheerfully given as you may prescribe."

In the issue of the *Illustrated Times,* dated 15 September, 1860, alongside an account of Garibaldi's liberation of Naples, a criticism of the Suez Canal project, and a reported alliance between England, Austria and Prussia against France, a column is devoted to a great review by Lord Derby of the Lancashire Volunteers in Knowsley Park. The troops included the Lancashire Hussars, the Lancashire Mounted Rifle Volunteers and the Liverpool Brigade of Artillery " of which the first Battalion was under the command of Lt. Colonel Wm. Brown, formerly Member for South Lancashire, who was warmly greeted as he rode at the head of his troops. Nothing could, on the whole, be more admirable than the steady precision of movement displayed by the Artillery, particularly the first Battalion . . . " William Brown had always taken a lively interest in the Volunteer Movement and had organised the first Battalion with the help of two of his sons.

In 1856, to meet the need for a Free Library for the public of Liverpool, he contributed £100,000 to cover the entire cost of the building. Four years later it was presented to the Mayor with these words:

"I have been looking forward for some time to the present occasion, when everything connected with this establishment would be placed under the parental care of the Corporation. That day has arrived, and I have now the satisfaction of proclaiming that the library and museum are open to my fellow-townsmen and others, be their religion or their politics what they may. This is neutral ground. To see this building consecrated to the public good is most gratifying to me and consummates my utmost wishes and desires. To you, Mr. Mayor, I now deliver it over, for the perpetual benefit of the public, and especially my fellow-townsmen, earnestly wishing that prosperity, happiness, and every other blessing may attend you one and all."

His brother, James, came over from New York to be present at the ceremony. In the evening, at a banquet in St. George's Hall, a statue of William Brown was unveiled, a tribute not only to his generous gift, but to the fifty years of service he had given to his adopted city.

In the New Year's Honours List in 1862 a baronetcy was conferred upon him, Lord Palmerston informing him that it was "in consideration of your eminent commercial position and of your generous conduct towards the public of Liverpool with respect of the munificent gift you have made to them . . ." Two years later, in 1864, Sir William Brown died at his home at

Richmond Hill. None of his eight children survived him, and the baronetcy passed to his grandson, William Richmond Brown. He had lived to see the House he founded in Liverpool, in 1810, develop from a modest merchanting business into an important firm of Merchant Bankers, with a reputation second to none. He had seen it meet crisis after crisis, both financial and political, and emerge stronger than ever when the ordeal was over. Although there was no son to follow him in Brown, Shipley & Co., there was to be no break in the links that connected the firm to a distant past, as both F. A. Hamilton and Mark Collet were steeped in the same tradition.

CHAPTER NINE

BROWN, SHIPLEY & CO. AT FOUNDERS COURT

THE American Civil War can be said to have ended the merchanting activities of the Browns. It had most seriously affected Liverpool's cotton trade with America as, owing to the strictness of the blockade, shipments of cotton from the United States ceased almost entirely. As early as 1861 Mark Collet was urging upon the New York partners the need to open a London office. The Civil War had delayed matters but a proposal to establish an agency in Havannah revived the idea. Provided there was no rupture between England and America, following the *Trent* affair, the Havannah agency was to be concerned mainly " with foreign exchange and with other experimental business that may offer ". If, however, the two countries were at war, then (says Mark Collet, in a letter to Brown Brothers) " Havannah may become a point of vital importance to us in resuming our Southern business so soon as the Gulf ports are open. If cotton could not be shipped with safety direct to Europe no doubt it could freely go to Havannah for re-shipment in neutral vessels, and whether we were able to reopen our agencies in Mobile or New Orleans or not, Havannah would be an important point from whence to supply those agencies with funds, or for originating business based on the reopening of the Southern trade . . . " But the Civil War dragged on and, for a variety of reasons, Collet's plans did not materialise. One feels, however, that had it done so, and the merchanting business continued as before, it would have pleased F. A. Hamilton, who was wedded to Liverpool and to the cotton trade.

There was another factor that had to be seriously considered; this was the laying of the transatlantic cable that was to be in operation in 1866. This, more than anything else, put an end to the intervention of the merchant in the cotton trade as, following the successful establishment of cable communication, manufacturers in England, France and Germany bought their cotton by cable on samples previously sent to them from the various places of shipment—New Orleans, Mobile, Charleston, Galveston, Savannah, Memphis and other towns. The samples were sent by brokers in these towns, often accompanied by a firm offer price, and the cotton-mill owners could examine them carefully in their own offices, make their selection for the style of goods they manufactured in their particular mill, and cable either the acceptance of the offer or a counter-offer, with authority (usually arranged through some banker) to draw against shipment. The consequence of this was, for a time, empty warehouses in Liverpool, and warehouse property, which had brought in a good return to the owners, diminished greatly in value.

Until the general trade of the port had adjusted itself to the revolutionary change the mercantile community suffered severely, for not only did consignments of cotton and other produce for sale practically cease, so too, to a large extent, did the manufactured goods for export, which had previously been shipped through Liverpool merchants and were now shipped direct by the manufacturers to the buyers on a through bill of lading. The old mercantile firms that were the pride of Liverpool soon disappeared. They had to change their character altogether and adjust themselves to the change, or (as so often was the case) close down. Of course, Liverpool, with its unrivalled docks, continued to thrive, becoming one of the world's greatest shipping ports and also a great centre of insurance; but for Brown, Shipley & Co. the day of profitable mercantile business was nearing its end.

The merchant banking activities of the firm, however, were rapidly expanding and a London office became increasingly necessary if this business was to be handled economically and to the best advantage. Because of Sir William Brown's close ties with Liverpool, both Mark Collet and the New York partners were not disposed to press for this until, in 1863, Sir William himself gave his consent to the proposal. At first there were suggestions that the London office should open in a name other than that of Brown, Shipley & Co., but this was promptly ruled out, since it would have meant losing the enormous goodwill and prestige that the firm's name carried with it. Mark Collet found premises in Founders Court, Lothbury, facing the Bank of England, and leaving Hamilton for the time being in Liverpool, took charge of the London office.

The history of Founders Court is a romantic one. Excavations in 1927 revealed that Brown Shipley's premises stand upon the foundations of a Roman building of Hadrian's day (A.D. 117-138). Remnants of the walls were uncovered, built of excellent tile bricks and resting on piles which were still in an excellent state of preservation, their points almost as sharp as when they were first cut some nineteen centuries ago. The walls of the rooms had been plastered and painted in different colours, two in shades of red and one in yellow. On the east side of the Roman house a pavement of red and black tiles was discovered. It was about six inches thick, the small tiles being laid in fine mortar. Many Roman relics were found, including several fragments of Roman pottery, some dating back to the reign of Augustus, who died A.D. 14. There were also leather relics, such as pieces of leather jerkins, one bearing the name of the owner, who had cut into it the letters . . . ULIANUS with a sharp knife. There were ladies' shoes of small size, pointed at the toe and with low heels. One of them revealed that the wearer had had a corn on her little toe! There were the remnants of a Roman lady's beauty aids—part of an exquisitely coloured glass scent bottle, an ornamented wooden stick, probably used for applying kohl to the eyes, also a little boxwood spoon such as was used by the Greek and Roman ladies for extracting perfumed unguent (equivalent to the modern skin-food) from the pot or jar in which it was contained nearly 2,000 years ago. The most interesting find of all, and a great rarity among Roman relics in Britain, was a gold hairpin or possibly it may have been the pin of a brooch.

When the Bank of England was re-building a section of its premises, a brass alms-dish was discovered. Recently, during excavations on the King's Head site nearby, a similar brass dish came to light. There is a possibility that both dishes date from the time when the Brassfounders Company had their Hall on the Founders Court site.

Lothbury was the trade centre for the founders in the City of London. They made bells, weights and measures, and various utensils, also candlesticks, buckles, spurs and stirrups. The earliest record of the Founders' Company is a petition to the Mayor and Aldermen of the City, presented in 1365. They complained that there were some who were using bad metal and solder in their work. The articles made by these unscrupulous workmen cracked, broke, or dissolved when exposed to great strain or fire " *to the peril and damage of those who purchase them and to the great slander of the City and of the whole mystery* ". The Founders' Company obtained new ordinances in Henry VII's reign, in 1489, but they did not have a Hall of their own at that time. In the 16th century the industry was booming and they bought two houses and a garden close to the Church of St. Margaret, Lothbury, and here they built their new Hall. By 1549 a second Hall on the same site had been built and in 1584, when considerable alarm had arisen because of the loss of the legal standards, the Founders' Company was made responsible for the standard weights and measures and no person was allowed to buy or sell except with weights and measures that bore the stamp of the Founders' Company. Although weights and measures are now controlled by Acts of Parliament, the Board of Trade being responsible for observance of the standards, the rights of the Founders' Company have never been formally abolished. The beadle still has the power to check weights and has in his office in St. Swithin's Lane the necessary equipment for doing so; but the last entry in the Company's Weights and Measures Receipt Book is dated 1908.

Of Lothbury, John Stow, the chronicler and antiquarian, writing in 1598, says: "The Street of Lothberie, Lathberie, or Loadberie (for by all of those names have I read it), took the name as it seemeth of 'beri', or 'court', of old times there kept, but by whom is grown out of memory. This street is possessed for the most part by founders that cast candlesticks, chafing dishes, spice mortars, and such-like copper or laton works, and do afterwards turn them with the foot and not with the wheel, to make them smooth or bright with turning and scratin' (scratching, as some do call it), making a loathsome noise to the by-passers that have not been used to the like, and therefore by them disdainfully called Lothberie." Writing in Queen Anne's day, Hutton says: "Lothbury was in Stow's time much inhabited by founders, but now by merchants and warehouse-keepers, though it is still not without such-like trades as he mentions." In Ben Jonson's play, the "Alchemist", Sir Epicure Mammon says:

"This night I'll change
All that is metal in my house to gold;
And early in the morning will I send
To all the plumbers and the pewterers,
And buy their tin and lead up; and to Lothbury
For all the Copper."
"What, and turn that too?", asks Surly.

H

*" Yes, and I'll purchase Devonshire and Cornwall
And make them perfect Indies."* replies Mammon.
Tokenhouse Yard, leading out of Lothbury, is so named
from an old house that once stood there and which was
the office for the delivery of tokens, issued by many
London tradesmen as small change. Copper coinage, with
very few exceptions, was unauthorised in England till
1672. It was in Tokenhouse Yard that Sir William
Petty, one of the original members of the Royal Society,
built himself a house. A lineal ancestor of the Lansdowne
family, he compiled the first bills of mortality for his
neighbour, John Grant, and it was on the development of
his ideas that Dr. Halley, the Astronomer Royal, was able
to publish his table of probabilities of the duration for
human life at every age, thus providing the first
actuarial basis for life insurance. In the days before
London had its first piped water supply, a conduit from
which clear spring-water could be drawn is believed to
have stood almost opposite the entrance to Founders
Court.

After being destroyed in the Fire of London, the
Founders' Hall was rebuilt and for many years was let
for various purposes. Wilson, in his " Dissenting
Churches ", tells us that it had "a Scotch Church meeting
in it, there being but one more of the kind in England ".
The Scottish Presbyterian Church had been able to
establish itself in London during the time of James II.
Previously it had to meet in exile in Rotterdam. It was,
in fact, London's oldest Scottish Church, and as the
Browns were Presbyterians it was a remarkable coinci-
dence that Mark Collet should have chosen Founders
Court for Brown Shipley's London office. Wilson tells
us: " The Meeting House is situated at the top of
Founders' Hall Court, and is accessible by means of a
flight of stairs, the lower part being occupied by a
Tavern." In 1700 the " parlour " was let to a dancing-
master and for a century or more various rooms appear
to have been let off for a variety of purposes, but the

Dissenters or Nonconformists continued to hold services in the building until 1846, when it was leased to Ricardo's Electric Telegraph Company. In 1854 the Founders' Company, reaching their 500th anniversary as a Livery Company, decided to build new offices in St. Swithin's Lane, which building survived the bombing raids in World War II that destroyed so many halls of City Livery Companies. In 1854 the Founders Court property was reconstructed and it remains today much the same as when Mark Collet chose it as the London home of Brown, Shipley & Co. It is doubtful whether the historic background of Founders Court was even known to the firm at that time, and its main attraction was its ideal position, close by the Bank of England.

Once the London Office was ready the following circular letter was sent out by Brown, Shipley & Co., Liverpool, on 15 December, 1863:

We beg to inform you that we have opened a house in London under the same firm as that in Liverpool. The business will be conducted at both places in connection, as hitherto, with our establishments in New York, Boston, Philadelphia and Baltimore. The address in London will be

Founders Court,

Lothbury,

London, E.C.

When Mark Collet came to select his clerical staff he was at once faced with a problem. He had picked out five or six of the Liverpool clerks, including a bookkeeper and two bright apprentices, to form the nucleus. Hamilton, however, declared that they were indispensable to him at the Liverpool office and, with one or two exceptions, the staff at Founders Court had to be recruited locally. As London was somewhat ahead of Liverpool in methods of book-keeping and office routine generally, there was some friction between the two offices when Mark Collet insisted on the system in Liverpool being brought into line with that at Founders Court.

In fact, the difficulty was only resolved when the book-keeper in Liverpool was retired on pension. Incidentally, Brown, Shipley & Co. in those days paid their staff monthly, in advance. The same practice is followed today. The commencing salary of an indentured junior clerk was then £20 per annum, and the firm's prestige and the fine training given to its young men, were such that recruitment was never a problem.

For two years more, F. A. Hamilton remained in Liverpool with Stewart H. Brown, Mark Collet being joined at Founders Court by Herman Hoskier, from the New York office, and by Frederick Chalmers, who was married to Miss Edlmann, a sister of Mrs. Collet. (Both were later made partners—Herman Hoskier in 1866, and Frederick Chalmers in 1872.) When, in 1866, another great panic swept the City, bringing down, among others, the important firm of Overend, Gurney & Company, it became desirable for F. A. Hamilton to be transferred to London, Frederick Chalmers then moving to Liverpool. Fortunately for Brown, Shipley & Co. they were not involved in the crisis, and in the words of Herman Hoskier (to whom it always came much more naturally to write in French than English), " *Depuis le commencement de la crise nous n'avons pas escomté un sou, et, à l'exception de Rothschild et Baring peut être, je crois que personne ne peu dire autant* ". They were, none the less, difficult days for Mark Collet, although this was not the sole reason for requiring his old colleague at his side. That year, only two years after he had opened the office at Founders Court, he was elected a Director of the Bank of England, of which he was to be Deputy Governor (from 1885 to 1887), and Governor (from 1887 to 1889). He wanted Hamilton's mature judgment to be available at Founders Court when he himself was on other duties. Writing, in 1900, Sir Mark Collet (on whom a baronetcy had meantime been bestowed for his services in connection with the conversion of the National Debt) says:

" I was elected a Director (of the Bank of England)

in 1866, just before the great crisis of that year when Overend, Gurney & Company failed, and I am still on the Court, having filled the office of Deputy Governor and Governor for the usual term of two years each. The latter period embraced the conversion of the National Debt by Mr. Goschen, as Chancellor of the Exchequer, entailing upon the Governor, as well as the permanent staff, a very severe strain. I was for weeks in constant communication with Mr. Goschen preparatory to his making his speech, and indeed in formulating the whole plan. The labour it involved put such a strain on both myself and two or three of the higher permanent staff that our health gave way, and that was the beginning of my breakdown . . . I accompanied Mr. Goschen to the House (of Commons) where I had a seat in the Speakers' Gallery, and had some difficulty, before he took his seat, to keep him up to one point on which he feared to be attacked, but which, if he had yielded upon, would, I feel sure, have impaired, if not wrecked, his scheme. I joined him in his private room in the House after the debate, when he thanked me warmly for the services that the Bank had rendered the Government; and some time after (wholly unsought and unexpected by me) I was offered through him a baronetcy in recognition of those services.

In looking back, I remember with gratitude that having taken a more or less active part in all the great commercial panics of the last sixty odd years, and in the business that led up to them, I have been preserved from any more serious consequences to myself than the anxiety involved . . . but remembrance of (them) remains too vivid ever to pass from my memory."

It was not easy for F. A. Hamilton to adjust himself to conditions in London. He was no cosmopolitan. His one relaxation was hunting, and to forgo his days with the Cheshire Hunt was something of a sacrifice. Unlike London, where most transactions, whether financial or commercial, were arranged through brokers, his business in Liverpool, particularly in the cotton trade, had meant contact with the principals. Those with whom he was dealing in the day-to-day transactions of the firm were well known to him and many were close friends. In short, he knew everyone in the mercantile life of that city but, with the exception of Sir Mark Collet, he found himself a stranger among strangers at Founders Court. He knew no one in the City and no one knew him, but a man with such sterling qualities and such marked ability was bound to make his mark and before very long those qualities were recognised. Thus, in 1871, when Sir John Lubbock introduced a Bill in the House of Commons modifying the law with regard to Bank Holidays, it was Hamilton who succeeded (after it had been read a third time, and had gone to the Lords) in having the Bill altered so that Bank Holiday included Acceptance houses or Merchant Banks. His letter and the reply of the Marquis of Salisbury on the omission, the implications of which had escaped the notice of all other Merchant Bankers, ran as follows:

"Having noticed that your Lordship has taken charge of the Bank Holiday Bill, I have to ask you to excuse the liberty I now take in pointing out a few of the serious inconveniences and complications likely to arise in Mercantile transactions, if the Bill passes in its present form.

The Bill provides for a 'Holiday for Bankers', and for the regulation of the payment of Bills of Exchange, Promissory Notes, etc. falling due on such Holiday, but it makes no such provision for a Holiday for Merchants, or acceptors of Bills.

Your Lordship is doubtless aware that there are many Houses, such as Messrs. Rothschilds, Baring Brothers & Co. and my own firm Brown, Shipley & Co., who are not legally Bankers, but Merchants, tho' their transactions in Bills of Exchange, Home and Foreign Monetary operations are on a much larger scale than many Bankers.

By the law, as it now exists, and will exist under the New Bill in its present form, these Houses will not dare to close their offices. They must present Bills for acceptance, attend to orders for Insurance, and make payments due otherwise than in Bills of Exchange and Promissory Notes. They will also be bound to protect all Bills not on Bankers, which may be unaccepted, in consequence of Offices being closed.

I may also point out to your Lordship that the Telegram is used to an immense extent in ordering payments of large sums on account of Parties in Foreign Countries, it being no uncommon thing to receive a Telegram ordering the payment on receipt of £10,000, £50,000, or even £100,000 in one line. How is this to be met?

A Merchant cannot retain in his Office sums like these to meet unexpected demands, and yet he is bound to carry out the contract made by his Representative abroad, who cannot be aware that his Banker is taking a Holiday.

By making the Holiday a legal one generally, and especially for Bankers, these embarrassments will be greatly relieved, if not entirely removed. At any rate no legal responsibility can be entailed on Merchants, if the Law includes all classes and not Bankers only.

The inconvenience of a want of uniformity in paying Bills under the old and new Holiday Acts is so apparent as scarcely to call for comment, were it not for the way the House of Commons has ignored it. I, therefore, merely give an illustration of the practical working of this Clause of the present Bill.

Should December 26th happen to fall on a Sunday, then Xmas Day being on Saturday, Bills due on the 26th must be paid in the previous Friday under the existing Law. If the 26th December falls on a Monday, then by the New Law, Bills due on this day will not be payable till Tuesday. This will be rather a difficult calculation for foreigners who have to provide for their engagements in this country.

I beg to apologise for trespassing on your time, and can only offer as an excuse the importance of the case, and shortness of time before the Bill may become Law."

To this the Marquis of Salisbury promptly replied (from Hatfield House):

"Lord Salisbury presents his compliments to Mr. Hamilton, and begs to acknowledge with many thanks the receipt of his letter in reference to the Bank Holiday Bill, and to say it shall receive his careful attention. He understands it is the intention of the Duke of Richmond to move to alter that portion of the Bill which makes bills payable on the day subsequent, instead of preceding, the day declared to be a Holiday."

It was regarded as a minor triumph for Brown Shipley and for F. A. Hamilton personally, that this glaring error in the framing of the Bill should have been detected in time and the City was not slow in paying tribute to his perspicacity.

Up to 1 January, 1874, by which date a change was made by the U.S. Treasury Department in computing the value of a sovereign or pound sterling, sterling exchange was quoted at a premium from the fictitious or arbitrary par—say, 4.44 to the pound sterling. The gold par of exchange, or the mint value of a sovereign represented in dollars, was, say, 4.8665 to the pound, and was expressed by a premium of about $9\frac{1}{2}$ per cent. from this fictitious par. At the time of the Civil War and in the years following, there were violent fluctuations and no one could tell what the premium on gold would be within the next twenty-four hours. The highest prices for both gold and sterling was reached in 1864 when, on 13 July, it is on record that a good line of Brown Brothers' sixty-day bills on Liverpool was sold in currency at 8.06, representing a premium on gold of about 172 per cent! Some of these bills were bought back again, a few days later, at fifteen or twenty points less. A prospective buyer regarded the Browns' 60 days' Sterling Bills on Liverpool as the equivalent of gold, knowing that they would be paid in Liverpool in gold sovereigns at maturity.

Although such extreme rates lasted only a short time, it illustrates the rapid fluctuations and the consequent difficulties with which all foreign business was transacted. When, by act of Congress, the rate was fixed at four dollars eighty-six cents and six and one-half mills as the value of the sovereign or pound sterling, the new method of quoting exchange had a very marked effect in reducing the margin between buyer and seller; but it also gave a real impetus to foreign trade. There were other changes taking place that would have surprised the earlier partners. In the old days it was the strict practice of the Browns to limit the amount of credit given to any one firm, no matter how good they happened to be, and also to ensure in all cases that the goods remained under Browns' control until they reached England or America, as the case may be, and then to deliver to the merchant such an amount as his credit at that time warranted. Thus, in the event of failure, the loss with any one firm was never serious, and there are scores of letters that tell the story of escape from disaster through rigid adherence to this practice. It was never the policy of Brown Brothers or of Brown Shipley to build up a mammoth business. (" *Be content; we are doing well enough* ", counselled the Founder to his son.) Baring Brothers & Company, on the other hand, refused to grant credits unless they could have all the business, and then only to men or firms in a large way of business and with established credit, to whom consignments of goods could be shipped direct. When all was well the profits were large; but one or two failures could involve them in very serious losses. The size of a business and the money behind it has never been the only yardstick for Brown, Shipley & Co. when considering the granting of credits. Many a man of character who, through some understandable misfortune, was without the necessary funds to exploit a profitable enterprise, has had reason to be grateful to Brown, Shipley & Co. for the accommodation he was given. But changing conditions demanded a less rigid application of these two different credit policies. As trade increased, the volume of business in some cases became too great for any one Merchant Banker to handle in its entirety. At the same time, speed in transport and communications, including the establishment of an international cable service, necessitated an earlier release of goods. A more flexible attitude was developed, to meet the genuine needs—not necessarily the demands—of the customer.

Some doubtful propositions were being put up to the British investor at that period. A glib tongue and a handle to one's name was the stock-in-trade of most of the share-pushers, and if they were able to secure one or two good names as directors of an enterprise the task was all the easier. Many adventurers made the crossing both from and to the United States to raise money for all sorts of projects, many of them of a questionable character. The old letter-books have several references to them, and Brown, Shipley & Co. were quick to warn their New York partners when convinced they were being victimised. Alternatively, Brown Shipley would be given a confidential assessment of a man or a proposition if Brown Brothers sensed a possibility of the English house getting involved in a similarly questionable proposition. This letter, for example, may well have saved George Brown in Baltimore from loss:

" We notice that General W. wishes you to come on the direction of some Coal Mine as an inducement to others. We hope you will not in any way commit yourself until you hear from your brother, for we are satisfied he (the General) is not a man with whom you would like to be connected. In strict confidence, we would say he is an unprincipled scoundrel and a man on whose assertions and statements not the slightest faith can be placed. He is a man with little or no influence with the Government and it has always been a marvel to us how Lord E. would admit him to his house. We do not think, from what we have heard, that either Mr. James Brown or Mr. Stewart Brown would have him at their table. We can only suppose that by his gift of boasting and impudence, with some degree of talent maybe, he has forced people in this country to think that he is a man of some importance at home (i.e. in America), which is not the case. We have not the slightest doubt in our minds that this is his true character, and it is therefore safer not to commit yourself to any assertion he may make until you have this opinion refuted or confirmed. For one colliery that has done any good in the United States there are dozens that have gone wrong. You do not mention the name; can it be the great New York coal concern called the Dauphin? We should be extremely sorry to see your name with W's in America . . . no man can stand much lower, and as for influence we believe it counts for nothing . . . "

The interchange of confidences between the English and American partners enabled the House to avoid many pitfalls. Men like Howard Potter at the New York office, for instance, could always be relied upon for accurate information and the soundest of views on almost any financial project that emanated from that country. New York at that time was the breeding ground of strange theories, fermented by pseudo-economists and demagogues, and one had to step warily. Brown, Shipley & Co. were also in the happy position of being able to advise the New York office of the attitude of influential City men to American financial operations. As a two-way information service it was invaluable. Thus we find Herman Hoskier writing to Howard Potter on

29 December, 1879 regarding U.S. Funding operations:

"It is a curious thing that just after writing you on the subject of U.S. funding operations, I should have had the chance of speaking with Sir Nathan Rothschild on the subject, and I am happy to say in a manner quite in accord with our ideas.

I was over at the Bank of England, making a transfer, when I met Sir Nathan on the same errand, and curiously enough he was transferring £20,000 Consols into my name. This gave rise to a little banter between us, and we ended by a conversation on American affairs, which gave me the opportunity of saying: 'Are you at all thinking of doing anything in view of the next funding operations?'

Sir Nathan (who, you will understand, is now the Head of the House in England—he has *la haute main*) did not hesitate a moment, but replied, word for word as near as I can convey the words, 'With you I have no objection whatever to tell you exactly how the matter stands as far as we are concerned. Belmont (Rothschild's Agent in the U.S.) wrote me lately on the subject, and after consulting our Paris friends, I wrote back by last Tuesday's Mail, to say that we were ready to go into the matter, and would willingly take hold of it, but on one condition only, that we were not willing to join any American Syndicate and be at their mercy or command, and would only take it up if we were given the lead to work it our own way with a group of friends around us, as in my father's time—to which, of course, I have no reply'.

I thanked Sir Nathan for his confidence and frankness and said that, curiously enough, we had this very week expressed to you our decided disinclination to join any American Syndicate such as he referred to, and unless we had the lead ourselves we were only disposed to take a hand with his firm at the head, as in old times when, unfortunately we were not met.

Sir Nathan is a man of variable temper but an excellent man of business, and we are pleased to have had this conversation with him.

We were both busy and I left him immediately after the above, not however before saying: 'Being in correspondence on the whole subject with our partners in New York, do you object to me mentioning to them what you have told me?' His answer was about as follows: 'No; you may tell them; and if they would like to see Belmont about it we should be only too glad to work with a House of such eminence as Brown, Shipley & Co.'

With a simple 'Thank you' on my part, we parted, and I have really nothing to add . . . I only hope you are satisfied, as I am, with having sown seed in such a way.

Sir Nathan made one remark which I should like to record: 'I am not going to put myself in the position of having Bills put out on me for some fabulous amount, without any control on my part' (as if he had had sufficient experience of this!!). 'It is all very well when things seem smooth all round, but if things are not so, it would be a very different matter.' Thus showing that they further agree with us as to prudence being the better part of valour, and the primary consideration.

I have great pleasure in writing you the above—of course, all details in confidence for yourself and partners. On this side Mr. Hamilton and Chalmers have seen it. Mr. Collet is absent."

After 21 years with the Browns, first in Mobile and then, for 16 years, in London, Herman Hoskier retired from the firm on account of ill-health. On recovery, he continued, in a consultative capacity, to assist not only the Browns, but also Morgans, Barings and Hambros. In 1887 he was made a director of Guinness's Brewery and took a large part in the financial management of that concern. He was very proud of this association, and never tired of asserting that this was no ordinary Brewery but that fifty per cent. of its product was used medicinally. The latter years of his life were tragic ones. He lost his wife and daughter in the great fire at the Charitable Bazaar in Paris in 1897, and his only son in the Boer War.

CHAPTER TEN

THE LINK WITH LIVERPOOL IS BROKEN

SENTIMENT dies hard, and despite the fact that the Liverpool office was losing money steadily, year by year, it was not until 1888 that it was finally closed and all business transacted at Founders Court. From 1859 to 1875 the profits of Brown, Shipley & Co. had averaged £104,000 a year, due in no small measure to the opening of the London office. They could have been very much higher, but the partners were content to keep to well-tried paths rather than break new ground, except for a conservative investment business. This development had been initiated by Brown Brothers, with John Crosby Brown and Howard Potter responsible. When the latter came to Founders' Court and stayed to make London his home for many years, he handled the investment side of the business. The largest profit in any one year in the last century was £237,499 in 1889—the first year following the closing of the Liverpool office. In only two years was there a loss—£20,000 in 1893 and £23,000 in 1896. Considering that 1893 was a year of financial crisis in England, the loss was a trifling one.

In 1875 a Brown was once more a partner in Brown, Shipley & Co. This was Alexander Hargreaves Brown, a grandson of Sir William and, like him, he divided his interests between banking and public life. He was to serve continuously for 38 years as a Member of Parliament and, like his grandfather, was to have a baronetcy conferred upon him. Unlike the American Browns, whose progeny staffed a business that extended from Baltimore to Philadelphia, Philadelphia to New

York, and New York to Boston, the fact that all Sir William's sons had predeceased him accounts for only six of the family being partners in Brown, Shipley & Co. in the century and a half that followed its foundation. There have, however, been few periods in the firm's long history when at least one of the partners was not a descendant of Sir William Brown and in fact a great-great-grandson of the Founder is a director to-day.

In the course of destroying some papers recently, a firm of City solicitors came across a letter from Brown, Shipley & Co. dated 3 January, 1871. It gives an interesting sidelight on the method then followed when sending cash by post. This was, of course, before envelopes were in general use, the letter being folded and sealed with wax. It concerned the request from a gentleman in Brighton for the balance of cash on deposit with Brown, Shipley & Co. to be sent to him. The letter from Brown Shipley reads as follows:

We are in receipt of your letter of yesterday, and in compliance with your request we enclose the ' First' halves of Bank of England Notes for £145, also our cheque on the London & Westminster Bank for £3 19s. 1d., as per memorandum at foot, say together £148 19s. 1d., the balance of the £250 deposited with us.

Please acknowledge the receipt of the ' First' halves of the notes, and the cheque, to us and we will forward the ' Second' halves of the notes.

Although sent by registered post, the added precaution of cutting bank notes in two and sending only the halves, was a routine practice in those days.

Despite safeguards such as this, it did not prevent Brown, Shipley & Co. being swindled by two members of their own staff on one notable occasion. Let the following letters to Brown Brothers & Company, New York, from Mark Collet—the first dated 14 January, 1879—tell the story:

" We sent you the following telegram this afternoon, *Private and Confidential—Our credit clerk A— C— in connection with E— W— have robbed us to the extent of £5,000, at present discovered, absconded, perhaps to America. Beware also of G. C. B— who held our Travelling Credit 12563 drawer your remise 25th September, supposed confederate.*

We are, of course, vexed and annoyed beyond our power of expression at having to send you such a telegram as that, and the worst of it is that we cannot yet say for certain that we know the extent of the frauds practised upon us, although two of our partners were here at the office till 3.30 p.m. Sunday afternoon and 10.30 p.m. last night, investigating the matter. We are still continuing our scrutiny and will advise you promptly of anything we may discover.

Both of the young men had been with us a long time, having been apprenticed in this office. A. C— came here in January 1864 and was promoted to the head of our Credit Department in 1872. He was a young man of considerable ability and did the work very quickly and intelligently. His handwriting must be very familiar to you in the letters, written to you from his Department—the last letter he wrote to you in that capacity was our 2 & 3 per *s.s. Batavia,* 28 December. On that same day he left on leave of absence for a week, having complained of feeling rather knocked up and unwell. He was due back January 6th but did not return, and we heard incidentally that he had left his lodgings on the 2nd January, paid the rent of them, and said he was going to New Zealand.

On Saturday last, 11th inst., Mr. Hoskier received a letter from him (without date or address, postmarked London), admitting that he had robbed us and expressing regret for having done so.

On looking very closely into the books we find that as long ago as 1875, a Travelling Credit was issued to

I

H. F. Hood for £500, purporting to be against securities lodged with us, which never had any existence in fact, and which, together with another subsequent credit for the same mythical person, seems to have been availed of by A. C. himself drawing through the West End branches of the London & Westminster and the London & County Banks.

Again a credit was issued to a Miss Perot, the record being that Mr. Hoskier had directed no redrafts to be sent till the credit was returned, then to redraw on Mr. John Crosby Brown ; whereas Mr. Hoskier knows nothing of any person of that name and is very sure he gave no such instruction.

Another credit was for £250 in favour of G. C. B—, referred to in our telegram, and was availed of in our office in August for £50 and in yours for £200 in September last—(you returned the credit with the draft)—Our book records that the credit was issued on the guarantee of S— B— who deny all knowledge of G. C. B— and we can find no trace of any such guarantee. Lastly, in the account of Mr. R. G. T— we find an entry for £50 advance in December, 1877, the draft for which does not appear ever to have gone forward. In all, we have discovered something like £1,400 which appear to have been fraudently obtained by C—.

E. W. has been with us since August, 1865. He was a quick, smart young man who could do his work very well when he chose to do so. We thought him careless and inattentive sometimes, but never suspected him of being dishonest. He did not come as usual yesterday morning and being rendered suspicious by the fact of his known intimacy with C—, we at once put ourselves in communication with his father and found that he had not returned home, and had sent mendacious telegrams to his wife to account for his not doing so. We then went over the Bills and compared them with the Books, when we found that, by

fraudulent entries, he had sought to cover a deficiency
of £3,700. We cannot yet say precisely how the money
was procured because the Bills were balanced, month
by month, and were called over as recently (by
Mr. Chalmers) as the 1st inst., but the deficiency is, we
fear, only too true—the Bills in the Diaries for
£1,500–£1,500 due today, and £700 due 11 February,
being not only absent but marked as entered on folios
which are either blank or contain only past due
Bills . . . We will advise you of anything else that
transpires . . ."

Serious as were the revelations, there was to be a
pleasurable experience for one member of the staff. A
clerk who had been far from well was detailed to
accompany a Detective Sergeant to Algoa Bay (Port
Elizabeth) to identify A. C. who, it was believed, intended
to start sheep-farming out there on his ill-gotten gains. It
had meantime been discovered that some of the stolen
notes had been used to pay for four passengers to Algoa
Bay, on the steamer *Nyanza*. Two were so-called
" brothers " giving the name of Myers; one was a man
called Bagney; the fourth was a Capt. S., a well-known
South African emigration agent, who had been advertising
in the English newspapers that he could find sheep farms
out there for young men with some capital.

By 8 March came news of the other culprit, W., as
Mark Collet's letter to the New York office reveals:

" We have now to inform you that the Detective
Police, having discovered that communications were
kept up between W. and one of his former associates in
this country (not in this office), by means of
advertisements in the *Standard* newspaper, followed
up the clue thus afforded, and eventually succeeded in
effecting his capture. We have a telegram this morning
to say that he is in custody at Rouen in France. By the
terms of the Extradition Treaty between England and
France, he must be kept there for 15 days before he
can be delivered over to the custody of the English

Police, but at the end of that time we hope to be able to report to you that he has been brought before the Magistrate to be committed for trial for embezzlement and forgery.

We are very pleased to add that you know already the worst of his defalcations."

Both A. C. and E. W. got their deserts, but this was no very real satisfaction to Brown, Shipley & Co. The defalcations came as a great shock to the partners at Founders Court. The realisation that there were black sheep in the fold was a bitter blow to their pride. One result of this unfortunate affair was the abandonment of old methods of recording transactions, and the adoption of more modern methods of accounting.

There were evidently black sheep also in a nearby office in Founders Court. In May, 1873, a projected new loan for the Canton Company was brought out by dubious neighbours named Bischoffstein & Goldsmid, in which Brown, Shipley & Co. were asked to take a share, but declined. In due course there arrived through the letter-box of the bank—anonymously, as was often the case in those days—a printed broadsheet, setting out in the most forthright fashion the writer's opinion both of the proposed loan and its sponsors. As a result, Mark Collet wrote to the New York office:

" Although this paper is only a ' skit ' it nevertheless shows the *mauvais odeur* in which the firm indicated is held, and how very easily ' Founders Court ', which is now synonymous with ' Brown, Shipley & Co.', here, might come to have a significance the reverse of all we should desire.

Of course the various innuendoes and hits in the ' skit ' would have neither point nor sting in them, and would be quite unworthy of our mention or your notice, were it not that in fact they are only thinly disguised descriptions of what has actually been done. In short, tho' clearly libellous, they are unfortunately true.

116

In all the circumstances, I think it well you should see it."

That good name, the very hall-mark of Brown, Shipley & Co., was something to be jealously guarded.

When dealing with the American Civil War and its effect on the fortunes of the Browns, reference was made to the dispute over the *Alabama*. This ship had been built at Laird's yard at Birkenhead and was intended as a man-of-war. Despite the fact that the British Government had issued a proclamation of neutrality, she was allowed (either by accident or design) to sail for the Azores, two British ships following with armaments. After fitting out she was then handed over to the Confederate government and until it came to an end in June, 1864, she had a most destructive career in attacking the commerce of the North. The United States Government regarded the supply of the ship as a flagrant breach of neutrality and claimed substantial damages. In 1871, after seven years of correspondence on the subject and much ill-feeling on both sides, a Commission was set up to determine how the issue might be settled. The Commission suggested that it be submitted to arbitration, but the Americans claimed that there had been such "insincere neutrality" on the part of Britain, and such "veiled hostility" shown in diplomatic correspondence during the Civil War, that damages should include not only the property destroyed by the *Alabama*, but also "indirect losses". Eventually, in 1872, the claim went to arbitration, and damages totalling $15,000,000—about $3\frac{1}{4}$ million pounds—were awarded to the United States Government, to the great indignation of a large section of the British press and public. Payment was due the following September, and in April of that year (1873) Brown, Shipley & Co. addressed the following letter to the Chancellor of the Exchequer:

" Sir,

Seeing the uneasiness and to our mind unnecessary alarm, which prevails in the monetary world, in reference to the *Alabama* payment in September next, you will perhaps excuse our addressing you on the subject.

You are probably aware that the long connection of our firm with the Commerce of the United States, and in which we are so largely engaged, has given us a great control over the Exchequer, and we feel fully satisfied that we could, under any ordinary circumstances that are likely to occur, transfer to Washington the amount due in gold, without causing any material inconvenience to the Mercantile Community, or derangement in the Money Market, and at the same time place the Government in the most advantageous position as regards the cost of transmission.

We should feel a much greater interest in carrying out the operation with success than in any benefit we might have expected to derive out of it, as a greater pecuniary advantage might easily accrue to us should the payment be made otherwise than through our intervention.

Should you wish to speak to us in reference to the question, we will wait on you at any time you may desire, and under any circumstances you can command any information we may possess, should you consider it of use."

An immediate reply was received from the Chancellor, enquiring the terms for transmitting the *Alabama* indemnity and asking when Brown, Shipley & Co. would require the money. F. A. Hamilton went at once to Downing Street to see the Chancellor (Mr. Lowe), who asked him " to make a tender for it ". Brown, Shipley & Co. suggested that the three and a quarter million sterling should be shipped—in sovereigns—by weekly instalments of £250,000, and at the rate of exchange prevailing. If the full payment of the indemnity had to be completed by 1 September, the first instalment would have to be paid to Brown, Shipley &

Co. on 19 May, thus allowing two weeks for transportation. Brown, Shipley & Co. suggested that the *modus operandi* be as follows: — The Chancellor of the Exchequer would give to Brown, Shipley & Co. a cheque for £250,000 on the Bank of England, every Monday before noon, Brown, Shipley & Co. giving an undertaking that their New York house would place gold, or U.S. Treasury Gold Certificates, in the hands of the British Minister at Washington, or hold it subject to his order. The British Minister would then telegraph the Chancellor, advising him that the payment had been made. (The " Gold Certificates " referred to are the U.S. Treasury acknowledgment that they hold a certain amount of gold coin at the disposal of the holder of said certificate.)

Brown, Shipley & Co. undertook to transact the whole operation for a commission of one half of one per cent. and expenses incurred, giving the Exchequer every benefit in the rate of exchange, " and rendering a full and precise statement of the whole operation " when completed. They further advised that it would not be to the benefit of the Government or suit their New York house to lend the gold in America. " If on the other hand " (says F. A. Hamilton, in his letter to the Chancellor), " the Chancellor of the Exchequer prefers that a certain rate of Exchange should be fixed beforehand, Brown, Shipley & Co. think that they can arrange it in that way, but beg to point out that they would thus be obliged to base their calculations on a low range, to secure themselves from actual loss on the transaction." Realising that pertinent questions were likely to be raised in Parliament concerning the payment of the indemnity, Brown, Shipley & Co. suggested that the arrangement should be kept private for as long as possible. " Brown, Shipley & Co. feel sure ", the letter went on, " that they will at all times be able to justify the course pursued by the Government and be able to answer satisfactorily any questions that may be raised in

Parliament or elsewhere." Eventually they offered " to effect the whole operation at the rate of 4.82½ dollars to the £ sterling, or 108 9/16 Exchange ".

To this letter they received a prompt reply as follows:

" The Chancellor of the Exchequer desires me to acknowledge with thanks the receipt of your letter of to-day's date, making an offer of the rate at which your firm would be prepared to undertake the transfer of the *Alabama* Indemnity. He will cause a further communication to be addressed to you."

Brown Brothers in New York had, of course, been kept fully advised of the plan and its progress, and a special secret code was devised for this purpose. There was a good deal of optimism on both sides of the Atlantic, and as F. A. Hamilton commented: " This prompt reply (from the Treasury) and the tenor of the last sentence does not leave us without hopes of securing the business, tho' we prefer not being over-sanguine!"

The days passed, but the promised letter from the Chancellor did not arrive. There were persistent enquiries from the New York office concerning the matter, and it was suggested that Hamilton should press for an immediate reply. His answer to this was typical: " We can do nothing for fear of appearing too anxious and spoiling our chance, whatever it may be!" A few days later, something happened in the City that dashed Brown Shipley's hopes. They realised there was a powerful rival in the field, and Brown Brothers were told of their fears: " The persistent purchases of drawn Bonds by Messrs. Rothschild make us feel very doubtful of getting the business." And so it finally proved to be (in angling parlance) " the one that got away ". It was, in fact, Messrs. Rothschild who eventually effected the transfer of the *Alabama* Indemnity.

CHAPTER ELEVEN

MONTAGU COLLET NORMAN AT FOUNDERS COURT

THE 19th century was ending. Brown Shipley's standing was as high as ever and Sir Mark Collet's position in the City lent it even greater prestige. It was inevitable, however, as in any long-established business, when a generation is nearing its end and a younger one is not ready to take its place, that there should be a certain reluctance to embark on new enterprises or to adopt new ideas. The partners were satisfied with the well-tried policy of the past and had no great desire to expand and even less inclination to experiment. This was not altogether surprising since (in 1894) F. A. Hamilton was over 80 years of age and, in fact, did not retire for another 10 years, and Sir Mark Collet was 79, and was to remain senior partner until his death ten years later.

There were at that time two other English partners. Frederick Chalmers, a brother-in-law of Mark Collet's second wife, and Alexander Hargreaves Brown, grandson of the founder, Sir William Brown. Chalmers had been in the Indian Army and had later studied for the Church, but before being ordained had left Cambridge to join Brown, Shipley & Co. He was in his 60th year (in 1894) and died suddenly three years later. Alexander Hargreaves Brown was 51, and devoted much of his time to his duties in the House of Commons which eventually earned him a baronetcy. In addition to the four English partners, there was the customary nominee of Brown Brothers, New York, this being John Crosby Brown, a grandson of Alexander Brown of Baltimore.

The work at Founders Court at this comparatively uneventful period was largely confined to giving acceptance credits to American customers of Brown Brothers; thus the really interesting part of the job—the examination of applications for credits and the gauging of credit worthiness—was undertaken in New York. In addition, Brown Brothers sponsored long-term new issues, and again it was the function of Brown Shipley to act largely as agents. There was, however, as always, a considerable foreign exchange business at Founders Court, and a certain amount of deposit banking. It was against this background that a young man who was to make history first came to Founders Court. His name was Montagu Collet Norman, and the story of how he came to join Brown, Shipley & Co. is an interesting one.

Sir Mark Collet had a son and a daughter. The son was never interested in banking as a career and lived with his invalid wife in the South of France for some years before settling permanently in the Isle of Man, which is still the home of the Collets. Sir Mark's daughter married the son of George Warde Norman, and it was upon his grandson, Montagu, that Sir Mark lavished his affection and pinned all his hopes and aspirations. The boy was treated more like a son than a grandson and spent his young days with his grandparents at St. Clere, their home in Kent, which in later life Norman was to acquire as his own home.

From Eton, Norman went on to Cambridge where, surprisingly, he made no great stir; indeed, after only one year, his tutor told him that there was no point in staying on as he could never hope to get a degree! They parted company, and neither could have envisaged the day when, as Governor of the Bank of England and one of the great names in international finance, he was to return to Cambridge to receive an honorary degree. Once he had left the University his real education began. First he went to Dresden, where he not merely learned to speak German fluently, but was able to indulge in his passion for music. A year later he was joined by his younger brother, and together they visited Prague, Vienna, Heidelberg and Beyreuth. He then went on alone to Switzerland, where he was able to perfect his French. His health was never robust, but the months he spent with the foresters in the woods and with the villagers in the fields did much to build up his physique.

In 1892 he returned home to start work and, as a son of a prominent banker and grandson of the senior partner in an international merchant-banking house, he started life with obvious advantages. Plans no doubt had long since been made for him to follow a banking career and Sir Henry Clay (in his biography of Lord Norman) says there was never any doubt in Norman's mind as to the profession he should adopt. On the other hand, there is ample evidence that the Army as a career attracted him and that, given a free choice, he might have been lost to banking, and certainly there were far more distinguished soldiers than bankers in his family. Filial duty was strong in him, and as a banking career was clearly expected of him it was to Martin's bank in Lombard Street that he first went. It is significant that, as soon as he was settled, he took a Commission in the Militia. In that same year (1894) he came to Founders Court. From its foundation Brown, Shipley & Co. has been much favoured as a training ground for young men intent on making banking a career and one such trainee, contemporary with Norman, was Edward Charles Grenfell. A cousin of Vivian Hugh Smith (the first Lord Bicester), he became a partner in J. S. Morgan & Co. (successors to George Peabody & Co. and known, since 1910, as Morgan Grenfell & Co.). E. C. Grenfell was for many years on the Court of Directors of the Bank of England and was raised to the peerage with the title of Lord St. Just.

Preliminary training in deposit banking, always a useful basis for ultimate training in merchant-banking, was invaluable, but once at Founders Court, Norman's initiation into the routine, a necessary but somewhat dull business, proved irksome and after only a few months

there he persuaded his grandfather, aided and abetted
no doubt by John Crosby Brown, to allow him to
transfer to the New York office. All his life he had the
urge to travel and was a great believer in personal contact
and in seeing things for himself. Up to that time, in all
the 84 years that the firm had been established, only
three visits had ever been paid to the United States by
the English partners: Sir William Brown's visit to
Baltimore to see his family in 1811, and that of F. A.
Hamilton and Mark Collet to New York during the
critical days of the American Civil War. Had it not been
for the practice of posting an American partner to the
London house Brown Shipley's only contact with Brown
Brothers would have been by exchange of letters and
(more recently) by cable.

Once in New York Norman found it just as irksome as
at Founders Court. He realised there was no short-cut
that would enable him to escape the routine training and
as he was never a good " mixer " and indeed all through
life was shy, introspective, and singularly inarticulate,
except with a few intimate friends, he was at first very
unhappy there. Club and hotel life never did appeal to
him and noticing how lonely he appeared to be, one of
the partners, Eugene Delano, took him under his wing
and invited him to his home. It was a warm gesture that
Norman never forgot. It was at the Delanos that he
first met that remarkable American actress Ruth Draper,
well remembered for her solo performances, without
scenery and with the minimum of " props ", that could
alway fill a theatre whenever she chose to visit London.
The two were to be close friends throughout their lives.

Before eventually returning to London, Norman was
able to see a great deal of the country and its people and
he liked their way of life. The experience in those
formative years made a deep and lasting impression on
him and had it not been for the Boer War he might well
have decided to make America his home; but his
obligations as a militiaman had first call and he soon

found himself on active service in South Africa. There he was fortunate in being able to use his initiative, and he proved himself to be a fine soldier and an able organiser and administrator, and although dogged by ill-health and invalided out of the Army, it was not before he had been awarded the D.S.O.

After a long period of convalescence he returned once more to Founders Court, having been made a partner in 1900. No longer could he complain (as he had once said of his work there) that he wanted " something more to do than keep an office stool warm ". There was plenty to engage his attention and he soon made his mark in the City. Seven years later he was elected a Director of the Bank of England and thus began an association that extended over 37 years, being re-elected as Governor, year after year, for 24 years.

Meantime Norman had his first real experience of financial crisis when, in 1907, yet another great Panic in America had its inevitable repercussions in London. There had been considerable speculation in America both on the Stock Exchange and in commodities and over 500 million dollars was borrowed by American institutions in Europe, a large proportion of this in Britain. The United States Treasury was forced to deposit substantial Government funds in the New York banks, following a reported deficit in reserves, and this caused great anxiety in London. The Bank of England reserves fell heavily and its bank rate rose from 4 per cent. to 7 per cent., a rate only reached (until then) on rare occasions, as for instance, in 1873 and in the crisis of 1866 and in the Boer War panic of 1899. In America the Westinghouse Electric Company failed for 34 million dollars, and the Knickerbocker Trust Company, with its deposits of $33\frac{1}{2}$ million dollars from 17,000 depositors, closed its doors. Runs followed on other Trust Companies and on many banks and continued for 14 days, depositors standing all night in the queue to get a chance of withdrawing their money the next day. In the train of American events came failures in London, Hamburg, South America and elsewhere; but for Brown Shipley and Brown Brothers, who had seen so much of this before and were ready for any emergency, there was no crisis and no serious loss; and apart from clearing banks, Brown Shipley's dollar cheque on Brown Brothers, New York was the only one acceptable in the City during the crisis. As events were to prove, all this was invaluable experience for Montagu Norman.

In the years that followed Sir Mark Collet's death and F. A. Hamilton's retirement, Norman was a regular visitor to New York. It was during Theodore Roosevelt's term as President that Brown Shipley had their first insight into " dollar diplomacy ". It concerned Nicaragua, where one revolution followed another and where there was a very real danger that a Nicaraguan Canal might be cut as a rival to the Panama Canal. The peso at the time was valueless and trade, even on a barter basis, was almost non-existent. Brown Brothers, in association with J. W. Seligman & Co., undertook to sponsor a loan for the purpose of currency reform and to establish a bank, headed by Americans, to manage the currency. Browns and Seligmans each advanced 750,000 dollars and the National Bank of Nicaragua was duly incorporated. From the diplomatic angle the plan was successful, a treaty being signed that gave the United States an option on a canal route through Nicaragua and the right to construct a naval base on the Gulf of Fonseca. It was not long, however, before Browns and their associates realised that Nicaragua had not the slightest intention of re-paying the loan (which had taken the form of One Year Notes at 6 per cent.) and it had to be renewed, year by year, at this rate. No security had been offered in the first place, but eventually, under pressure, the stock of the Nicaraguan Railroad and of the Bank of Nicaragua was handed over. At once there was an outcry in the American Radical press and the inevitable Senate investigation followed. Apparently no one at first would believe the truth—that Browns and their associates had

lent the money without security and at only 6 per cent.
interest. As one Mississippi senator put it: " You could
have come down to my State and got 8 per cent. on short
loans, with cotton as collateral, and with an ample margin
too." It took 13 years (from 1911 to 1924) before the
Nicaraguan Loan was finally paid off, principal and
interest, thanks very largely to the efforts of Mr. James
Brown in New York, but not before it had caused much
heartburning at Founders Court.

It was not the only venture that had been regarded as
a total loss. There was, for instance, the West Virginia
Debt, a large part of the certificates of which were held
in London and other European capitals. It dated back
to the Civil War, when part of Virginia seceded from
the State and threw in its lot with the North. Subject to
assuming its fair share (one-third) of the debt of Virginia,
the seceded part became the new State of West Virginia
in the Union. In 1871 the State of Virginia, desiring to
refund this debt, did so by issuing bonds for two-thirds
of the old debt and pieces of paper called " West Virginia
Debt Certificates " for the balance. These were ignored
by West Virginia, and British investors, resentful at the
repudiation of so many American State debts, pressed
Brown Brothers, through Brown, Shipley & Co., to get
the matter settled. John Crosby Brown, on his return
from Founders Court, took the initiative in forming a
Committee with the object of getting a majority of these
certificates deposited with Brown Brothers. At that time
they were selling at a few cents per dollar, but after
listing the first 6 million certificates, trading in Brown
Brothers' certificates started at $3\frac{1}{2}$. Finally, when a
majority of over 8 million had been deposited, the market
price (on the New York Stock Exchange) never fell below
$5\frac{1}{2}$; and, in fact, when at last the certificates were on the
point of being delisted, a high of $76\frac{1}{2}$ was reached. But
this, however, was not until 1920, when a suit was
brought in the Supreme Court by the Attorney General
of Virginia. It succeeded and is on record as the only

money judgment ever made by the Supreme Court against a sovereign state. West Virginia settled the debt by paying 1,062,000 dollars cash and 13,500,000 dollars in $3\frac{1}{2}$ per cent. 20-year bonds. There was full compensation for the Browns and for the Committee that had been dealing with the matter for so many years, and although interest could not be paid to investors, almost the whole of their holding was paid off. The settlement added considerably to the prestige of the Browns, not only in London and New York but all over the world. The firm had done exactly what Alexander Brown and his sons would have done; they had taken this stand not for themselves but for their friends. As William Brown had said in that memorable crisis of 1837, the bank's customers must never knowingly be involved in any unnecessary risk that might mean ultimate loss, and Brown Shipley's policy at all times has been to keep faith with their customers. The repayments of the Nicaraguan Loan and the West Virginia Debt are but two examples of that sense of commercial honour and absolute fairness in all dealings that are synonymous with the names " Brown Shipley " and " Brown Brothers ".

Among the documents that have survived at Founders Court is a list of charitable donations for the year 1896. Its wide range not only reflects the social problems of the times but gives one an insight into the character and outlook of the partners. Hospitals, particularly those catering for consumptives, are reminders that tuberculosis was then a great scourge. Donations to soup kitchens; charities for the relief of the aged and the poor; grants to local elementary schools and for the provision of a public library service; all give some indication of the progress that has been made during the past fifty years in the provision of social services. As one would expect of a firm that began as merchant venturers, seamen's charities are high on the list. It was a time of financial crisis, and the mention of a substantial donation to a newly formed

A LETTER BY BALLOON POST. (1870)

Sent during the Siege of Paris to Brown, Shipley & Co.

THE FIRST TRANSATLANTIC AIR POST. (1919)

By the R.34, from Brown Brothers & Co., New York to Founders Court.

FOUNDERS COURT

Brown Shipley opened their London Office at Founders Court in
December 1863. The building stands on historic ground and
Roman remains of A.D. 14 were discovered during excavations in
1927. In the 16th century the Founders' Company had their Hall
on this site.

Gold Standard Defence Association shows how seriously the crisis was regarded in the City. Of all the items in the long list, one is of special interest. It records the payment of a small pension to the cabby who had his stand at the entrance to Founders Court.

K

CHAPTER TWELVE

THE WEST END OFFICE IN PALL MALL

ON 14 May, 1824, Alexander Brown & Sons, Baltimore, addressed to Wm. & Jas. Brown in Liverpool the following letter:

"At the request of our mutual friend, Dr. Ashton Alexander, we introduce to you Mr. John M. Colston, of Virginia, who crosses the Atlantic in search of Health, and to see his Brother who lives in Paris.

We have also lodged a credit in his favour of 250 pounds sterling, or any part thereof, which he may require. Your civilities and attentions during his stay in Liverpool will oblige."

This is certainly the first record of a letter of credit issued by the Browns, and it marked the beginning of a side-line of the banking business that grew to enormous proportions with the development of transatlantic travel.

Possibly the earliest reference to the issue of letters of credit concerns the ancient Greek civilisation and dates back to the 4th century B.C. Later, the Roman banks also issued letters of credit to facilitate travel within the Empire, and from this Roman practice the bankers of Lombardy developed similar facilities. King John is known to have issued them to his agents, travelling to Rome, in 1202. Gerard de Malynes, in his "LEX MERCATORIA", published in the early 17th century, mentions letters of credit as a means of settling commercial transactions. A century and a half later, Boswell was in correspondence with his father, asking that credits be arranged in various cities for his projected Grand Tour.

These early examples, however, refer to credits arranged with specific correspondents. Apart from the Browns, who were the first in the field with circular letters of credit, there followed a reference in 1840 to forged letters of credit purporting to be issued by Glyn, Halifax, Mills & Co. (Glyn Mills), which were presented at various banks on the Continent before the fraud was discovered. Lawson's " History of Banking " (1850) has no reference to letters of credit, but J. W. Gilbart, in " Principles and Practice of Banking " (1871 ed.), mentions " Circular Notes, for the use of travellers on the Continent ", issued by London bankers. There is no record of joint stock banks building up their systems of correspondents until the end of the last century, and it is fairly certain that none of them issued circular letters of credit before that date. From the beginning of the 19th century Alexander Brown and his son, William, had correspondents of undoubted standing in many overseas countries and their files reveal countless entries referring to the issue of circular letters of credit. Browns were first in the field, and through the English house were able to obtain the most stable and highly regarded correspondents throughout the world. At first, when the number of travellers was limited and communication between the United States and the continent of Europe was infrequent, circular letters of credit were issued by the Liverpool house only. The American traveller would receive from one or other of the branches in his country a letter of advice and introduction. This he was obliged to present at the office of Wm. & Jas. Brown & Co. (later to be Brown, Shipley & Co.), where it was exchanged for a circular credit on the firm's London bankers, Denison, Heywood, Kennard & Co. As means of communication and the volume of travel increased, this inconvenient method was abandoned. Circular letters of credit were then issued by the American houses on Messrs. Denison, Heywood, Kennard & Co., with a duplicate advice to the Liverpool house.

The old letter-books contain numerous references to Letters of Credit. One of the most interesting, addressed to Brown, Shipley & Co., and dated 13 July, 1838, refers to Jerome Napoleon Bonaparte, nephew of the Emperor and son of the beautiful Betsy Patterson of Baltimore, daughter of William Patterson, owner of the estate now known as Patterson Park. The Emperor Napoleon's brother was a French naval officer and was visiting America in 1803 when he met and married Betsy. The Emperor, hearing of this, ordered him to return to France and threatened him with imprisonment. Hoping to win over the Emperor, Jerome took his attractive young wife with him to Europe. There, however, he deserted her, before her baby was born, and she returned to her parents in Baltimore. When the son grew up he settled there, and there are numerous references to business transactions between Alex. Brown & Sons and Jerome Napoleon Bonaparte in the bank's records. The letter of credit reads as follows:

" We have great pleasure in introducing to you Jerome Napoleon Bonaparte Esq. (grandson of your old respected Correspondent, the late Wm. Patterson of this City) who, with his family, intends visiting Europe and making you his Bankers during his stay there—we have ordered the transfer as noted below to his credit, which we presume have all been entered in conformity—Mr. Bonaparte expects funds to fall into our hands and which we are to remit you, quite as fast as he will require them, but should it so happen that he may require Two thousand pounds above the funds in your hands, you will please advance it to him. We have informed him you will open such credit for him as he may require. Hoping you will be able to make his visit and that of his family an agreeable one while in Liverpool."

In a further letter to Brown, Shipley & Co., dated 23 February, 1839, Alexander Brown & Sons state:

" . . . You will please transfer £87 10s. 7d. to the

credit of J. N. Bonaparte as cash May 24, next. We have been told he has gone to France with a view of offering for the French contract for tobacco. If he gets it at the present high prices it will ruin him unless the contract is at very high prices . . . "

When the Trans-Siberian Railway was being built in 1843 the Russian Government, having noted the successful building of the Baltimore & Ohio Railway, engaged the services of two Baltimore engineers—two brothers, Thomas and William J. Winans—to undertake the work. There are several letters from the firm's Baltimore house to Brown, Shipley & Co. on the subject of credits in their favour: Dated March, 1843 two of the letters were as follows:

" We have much pleasure in introducing to you Mr. Thomas Winans, the son of our friend Mr. Ross Winans, who is well known to you. Mr. W. is on his way to Russia where he may probably enter into the employ of that Government, and we have to request that you will furnish him with such credits as he may require for his travelling expenses to the extent of Two Hundred and twenty-five pounds. Mr. W.'s signature is annexed for your government, and requesting for him your attention while in Liverpool . . ."

An extract from the cover-letter reads:

". . . Thomas Winans, a son of Ross Winans, goes out in this steamer on his way to Russia where he expects to enter the employ of that Government as Superintendent of some of their Machine Shops connected with a railroad now in progress. We have given him a letter of introduction and credit on you for £225 and for whatever he may use you will draw on his father here."

Later, on 28 November, 1843, the Baltimore house writes to William Brown:

". . . Thomas Winans will draw on you from St. Petersburg for £125 which you will pay, drawing on his father, Ross Winans of this City, for the amount . . ."

That the letters of introduction and credit service of the Browns were greatly appreciated is revealed in countless letters. Sometimes that appreciation proved embarrassing as, for instance, when a lady, to show her gratitude, instructed a London jeweller to send a ring to each of the partners! This prompted Alexander Brown to write (18 December, 1828):

". . . With respect to the rings Miss D. is desirous of sending to each of our firm, we are gratified she deems us deserving of such attention, but the partners included in our firm being numerous, including Alex. Brown and his four sons, living in different places, and none of whom have ever been in the habit of wearing a ring, we would, if it would not give offence, prefer her not taking any further trouble in that business. We consider (it) a compliment quite the same . . ."

When the London house was opened at Founders Court, letters of credit were issued on the London firm, drafts under these credits being paid at Brown Shipley's bankers—the Westminster Bank (in which Denison, Heywood, Kennard & Co. was incorporated). From the outset, it was part of the service of the Browns to handle the travellers' mail. In the early days, when it was sent to the Liverpool house, it was held or forwarded by them as directed. As travel increased between the two countries, the record of the addresses of the travellers, which used to be kept by one clerk in one book, had grown to such proportions that a card-index was necessary. Where formerly only one clerk could use the one book, a staff was then able to deal with the mail expeditiously. In the old days a second clerk often had to be employed on night duty, but this did not prevent serious delays which often inconvenienced travellers. By the end of the century it was realised that the limit of accommodation for this service at Founders Court had been reached. Moreover, it was not possible to cope there with the increasing number of travellers who called, and, in any case, it was much more convenient for them to call at a West End office rather than journey to the City. Accordingly, in April, 1900, a branch office in the West End was opened at 123, Pall Mall. It proved to be a great convenience to the increasing number of travellers using the firm's circular letters of credit, and it soon became a recognised meeting-place and information centre for American travellers in London, many regarding it as a kind of club.

As many as 15,000 letters on one single day of the usual eight or ten week tourist season were handled, and from 300,000 to 350,000 during the year. On one memorable occasion, when four mails came in together, 25,000 letters were dealt with. A staff of thirty or more was employed at peak periods. It was not merely a question of re-addressing mail but of dealing with hundreds of letters of instruction, all of which it was of course necessary to record and check before any mail concerning them could be dealt with. Scores of cables for repetition; registered letters requiring special attention; and countless enquiries in person by travellers, had all to be disposed of day by day.

Despite the carefully worded instructions concerning this service, a printed copy of which was given to every traveller applying for a circular letter of credit, it was remarkable how many ignored the detailed instructions or omitted to give even the minimum information that would have enabled Brown, Shipley & Co. to carry out their wishes. Many customers had the same name, some of these having the same initials. It was the rule, when this happened, to send the mail to the one first accredited if there was no means of identifying one from another, with a request to return the letters to Pall Mall if by chance the letters were not for him. When (as on one occasion) uncle, travelling in China, received by mistake the letters meant for his nephew, holidaying in Paris, there were ructions! There were many cases of forms and other instructions being received without signature. Scores of telegrams were addressed merely to the telegraphic address of Brown, Shipley & Co. and others were too vague or indefinite for action to be taken. For example, what could one do with wires like this, when the sender's name and address were omitted?—"*Please wire me present address of Josias Pennington of Baltimore*"; or one signed "*Mary*", addressed to "*Brownship, London*", saying "*Don't arrive before Saturday morning.*" Perhaps the most amusing of all, again addressed to Brown, Shipley & Co. and giving no indication of the sender or of the lady for whom it was intended, read as follows: "*Will you marry me? Cable yes immediately.*" Despite every effort on the part of the staff, great numbers of telegrams and letters were held up at the Pall Mall office and it was customary to display them in a show-case. Many an irate traveller who stormed into the office to complain of non-delivery of his mail, looked very sheepish when confronted with the waiting telegram or letter, lacking the essential information that would have enabled the staff to forward it promptly. Attempts were often made by unauthorised people to have their mail dealt with through the Pall Mall office, but when it was found that they were not holders of letters of credit they were politely but firmly told that they had "no more right to have letters sent there than to Buckingham Palace!"

The West End was a happy hunting-ground for pick-pockets and confidence tricksters and more than one of the customers of Brown, Shipley & Co. were victims. For instance, one credit-holder's pocket was picked on a Saturday afternoon as he strolled in Hyde Park. On Monday morning the victim called in at the Pall Mall office to report his loss, by which time the thief had drawn £100 in Amsterdam. Many plain-clothes police were known to the cashiers. They would sit, unobtrusively, in the hall of the bank, pretending to read the *New York Times,* when on the look-out for a suspect, and occasionally their vigil was not in vain. Not all Americans were charming; there were times when a clerk felt more sympathy for the crook than for his victim. There was, too, a particularly objectionable customer who believed that she should have priority over others who had been patiently awaiting their turn at the counter. It was the pride of the cashiers that they could remember the names of travellers, even though a year had passed since last they had been in England. On this particular day she had asked the usual question of a clerk, new to the business: " Any letters for me? " " What name Madam? " he asked. She glared at him and then wrote the name on a slip of paper and handed it to him. " Stick that in your lapel ", she ordered, " it may help you to remember next time." Such people were in the minority and most travellers were full of praise for the service they received, and it was not uncommon for boxes of cigars and other presents to be given to the staff on Thanksgiving Day or at Christmas time.

There were idealists among the customers. One such was a well-known Boston playwright who spent a great deal of money trying to reform the " painted ladies " of Leicester Square. Believing somewhat ingenuously that their way of life was solely one of economics, he had quite a number to whom he paid a weekly allowance. There was much amusement each Friday when they called to cash their cheques. It was a worthy experiment, but before many weeks had passed the social reformer had realised that his confidence was grievously misplaced. He had found them still practising their profession!

Many personalities connected with the Theatre were familiar figures at 123, Pall Mall. Among them were Dame Nellie Melba, the great Australian soprano, and Ruth Draper, the American actress and friend of Montagu Norman. There were such great names in the world of entertainment as Maisie Gay; Doris Keane; Elsie Janis; Maxine Elliott and her sister, Lady Gertrude Forbes Robertson; Peggy O'Neill; and many others. Among the playwrights were John L. Balderston, author of " Berkeley Square "; and J. Hartley Manners, author of " Peg o' my Heart ", and his wife, Laurette Taylor, who played the name-part in the London production.

One customer will be remembered as the donor of three " Spitfires " to the nation in the critical days of 1940. This was Lady McRobert, daughter of the Himalayan explorer, W. Hunter Workman, who had lost her three sons, flying with the R.A.F. She called her gift " The McRobert's Reply ".

Travellers' Cheques have now made unnecessary the issue of Letters of Credit and the service that accompanied it which Brown Shipley had pioneered. The West End branch was closed down in 1955 but there are still a great number of travellers who remember this Mecca of Americans in London and recall with interest, and indeed with appreciation and real affection, their visits to 123, Pall Mall.

CHAPTER THIRTEEN

THE END OF THE ANGLO-AMERICAN PARTNERSHIP

IN the summer of 1914 the financial horizon was clear and there was certainly nothing on either side of the Atlantic to indicate that war was imminent. With the bank rate at 3 per cent., the Paris rate 3½ per cent., and that of Germany 4 per cent., the partners went off for their customary holiday with no thought of war. The Pall Mall office was experiencing one of its busiest seasons, thousands of American travellers passing through on their way to the Continent. The partners in Brown, Shipley & Co. at that time, in addition to the senior partner, Sir Alexander Hargreaves Brown, were his nephew, Edward Clifton Brown; James Leigh Wood; Lawrence Chalmers, the son of Frederick Chalmers; and Montagu Norman, just back from one of his periodical visits to the States. They were leisurely days and life at Founders Court went on much the same as it had done since the turn of the century.

When war came it took the City completely by surprise; indeed the first real warning only came on 30 July when the Bank Rate was raised from 3 per cent. to 4 per cent. On the following day it was put up to 8 per cent. and when, on the very next day—a Saturday—it was raised to 10 per cent. it was realised that this was indeed Crisis. For Brown Shipley the outbreak of war posed many urgent and desperate problems. The working of the credit system, of which London was the centre, depended on peace. It relied on continuity of business and the interdependence of the various agencies constituting it, and thus when that continuity was interrupted everyone was involved in the consequences.

If the foreigner could not remit, the firm that accepted his bills could give no further credits and could be quickly in difficulties when faced with outstanding liabilities. No plan for meeting a credit crisis had been prepared and no machinery existed (as it does to-day) for intimate and rapid contact between the City and the Treasury. As the indebtedness of continental countries piled up, day after day, the inevitable result would have been the failure of all Accepting Houses and Banks, once their cash was exhausted. To have paid out pound for pound in gold to depositors was impossible and so, to prevent the sudden demand for currency at every branch of every bank, the Bank Holiday was extended from Monday to Thursday (inclusive), thus allowing time for the emergency issue in large quantities of Government notes for £1 and 10s., each bearing the facsimile signature of the Secretary to the Treasury, Sir John Bradbury, by whose name they were soon to be familiarly known. Simultaneously, three enactments came into force which had a vital effect on business:

(1) The extension of maturing Acceptances for a month at a time;

(2) The closing of the Stock Exchange and the deferment of all payments and deliveries due thereon, thus avoiding panic sales and shrinkage of values, and preserving the many firms that dealt on foreign account and could not complete their bargains;

(3) A month's moratorium regarding all debts due on demand, thus relieving the Discount Market and similar houses from having to repay their loans.

London was owed money by practically every country in the world and the first aim was to collect her debts as quickly as possible from neutral countries. In correspondence with James Brown at that time Montagu

Norman was in critical if not pessimistic mood regarding the firm's future. He had already made up his mind before the outbreak of war that he would leave Brown, Shipley & Co. and therefore his explosive comments on what he chose to call " idiotic credits " that should never have been given, and " promiscuous securities of uncertain value and still more remote worth " with which, he claimed, the firm was saddled, were personal views that were highly coloured to match his mood and were certainly not borne out by the facts. As was later revealed, the full extent of the assistance Brown, Shipley sought under the Government and Bank of England scheme to help the merchant banks at that time, was a mere $2\frac{1}{2}$ per cent. Within a very short time relations with customers had been satisfactorily adjusted, and although (to meet the views of the newly formed Accepting Houses Committee) the Merchant Banks re-accepted all maturing acceptances, it was not long before Brown, Shipley & Co. were actively retiring these extended bills from the Discount Market, both for the sake of their good name and also to terminate the interest charge which was added to such bills.

That the business immediately before the 1914 War lacked the virility and selectiveness it shows to-day is fairly certain, and thus Norman may have to some extent been justified in his assertion (to James Brown in New York) that if the firm had been " conducting business on proper lines the present would soon yield a golden opportunity "; but this criticism applied just as much to the New York office as to Founders Court, and not least to Norman himself as being the one London partner really responsible for acceptance credits.

Of all the pressing problems that faced Brown Shipley and Brown Brothers at the outbreak of war, none was more urgent than that of the American travellers in Europe who held their Letters of Credit. With all banks in Britain and on the Continent closed, the immediate problem was how to get money to the thousands of travellers and organise their transport home. Men with their pockets full of bills found it impossible to get change, and a hundred pound note was as little use to them as a blank sheet of paper. A handful of silver, drawn (if they were lucky) from Cook's, was the limit of accommodation anyone could get, and therefore something drastic had to be done to relieve the desperate plight in which they found themselves. With commendable speed a contract called " *Plan for Gold Fund for use in cashing American Travellers' Letters of Credit* " was immediately drawn up in New York by a group that had financed most of the American travellers. Brown Brothers were prominent among the ten banks concerned, and a fund of six million dollars was created, this being paid to the Bankers Trust Company, of which Benjamin Strong was at that time President and Fred I. Kent Vice-President. Fortunately the latter was in London at the time and was able to direct the disbursement plan. Meantime, the United States battleship *Tennessee* sailed for England with a first consignment of $4\frac{1}{2}$ million gold (" Eagle ") dollars and these were deposited with the London City and Midland Bank—now the Midland Bank Ltd.—and a London Committee, with Edward Clifton Brown as Chairman, was set up to deal with the matter. Kent had cabled Strong that the Embassies were not the proper places to handle money and suggested arranging with the continental banks to effect the distribution. Morgan Harjes & Co. undertook to do this in Paris, one of Brown Brothers' partners going over to assist. The plan was to cash a strictly moderate amount for each traveller, no more than sufficient to pay for food and lodging, and, when transport became available, a sum sufficient to pay for the passage home. The whole plan worked admirably and, as far as is known, no American traveller was left stranded in Europe and certainly none who held Browns' Letter of Credit. The major difficulty was in helping travellers who were in Germany and Austria when the war broke out. It had been decreed by the German

Government that no one would be allowed to leave, but after several weeks it relented and allowed them to leave the country. In contrast to the other European banks, it was then found that the German banks had been most liberal and had paid out generously for their weekly needs. It was a deliberate policy that paid handsomely as many travellers, once they were back home in America, proved to be very pro-German as a result of the kindness and consideration they had received at the hands of the Germans. The whole Gold Fund plan was a major triumph for the Browns and their associates and not only was no one left stranded, but all were full of praise for the Browns' service.

Brown Brothers also played a leading part in various measures that were urgently needed for the protection of credit and for financial aid for both Britain and France. A Marine Insurance bureau was set up in America under government auspices. Plans were also made to safeguard effectively the sterling-franc-dollar exchange, resulting eventually in the formation of the Gold Pool. A Treasury Commission consisting of Sir George Paish and Mr. (later Sir) Basil Blackett was sent to America to establish closer financial arrangements and to regulate the exchange, and twenty Presidents of National banks and Trust Companies, with several private bankers, met in Washington to consider the proposals and to make recommendations to the Federal Reserve Board. A committee was formed consisting of Albert H. Wiggin, President of the Chase National Bank; Benjamin Strong, President of the Bankers Trust Company; and James Brown of Brown Brothers & Company. Within two months of the outbreak of war their report was in the hands of the Federal Reserve Board. It was a measure of the Browns' status in the financial world that James Brown was sent to England to confer with the Chancellor of the Exchequer and the Treasury on their proposals.

It had been Montagu Norman's intention to retire from the firm almost immediately on his return from

America and although the outbreak of war delayed the final break it was clear that it could not be long deferred. Personalities had played a big part in the decision; he did not get on well with " Senior " (as he called Sir Alexander Hargreaves Brown) and as the latter had a great deal of his grandfather—Sir William—in him and was a very dogmatic and somewhat aloof person, differences of opinion between them were frequent. Norman's main criticism, however, was levelled against policy and, in particular, the issuing of securities and the underwriting of issues of other bankers. Although it was of course a perfectly proper activity, he claimed that the chief business of Brown Shipley as an acceptance house was in financing exports and imports by acceptances, and that all available capital was better employed in commercial banking. He never liked the idea of a merchant bank combining both commercial banking and security functions and although in the United States these dual functions had eventually to be divorced, following the American Banking Act of 1933, it has never been considered necessary in the City to insist on a similar division of activities. Had Montagu Norman been Sir Alexander's successor as senior partner it might well have been a different story. He was a man who was at his best when he was formulating policy and directing it. There is a story told that when Sir Henry Clay was appointed Economic Adviser to the Bank of England, Norman made it clear to him that he himself would do all the advising and that it was Clay's function to do the explaining! It was this difficulty in explaining his reasons for a particular view-point or decision that was so often, in the future, to be construed as obstinate refusal and in consequence he was frequently the target for a good deal of press criticism on that score. As a man, one either liked him immensely or disliked him intensely; there could be no half-measures. One is concerned here solely with the 20 years during which he was associated with Brown, Shipley & Co.; his brilliant record at the Bank of England, of

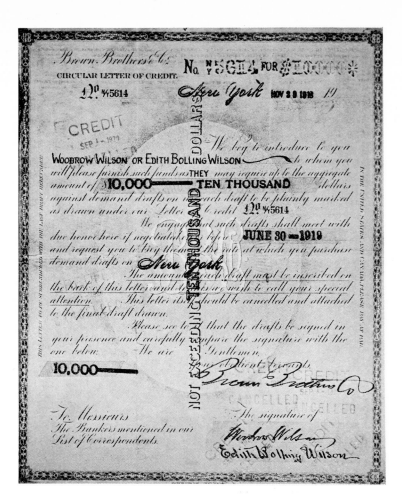

CIRCULAR LETTER OF CREDIT

Following the Armistice after World War I, President Woodrow Wilson (accompanied by his wife) crossed to Europe for the signing of the Peace Treaty, Brown Brothers & Co. providing a Credit of 10,000 dollars.

THE BROWNS' HOUSE FLAG

In their merchant days this flag, carried on the masthead of Browns' ships, was a familiar sight not only at Baltimore and New Orleans, Liverpool and Belfast, but at Havre, Lisbon, and other continental ports.

Their ships carried cotton for the Lancashire mills from the Southern States, returning with Irish linens and other manufactures to the States.

For a short period during the French Wars the Browns appear to have flown a red, white and blue striped flag, before reverting to their red and white flag.

which he was Governor for 24 years, owed much to that early training and experience in an Anglo-American merchant bank and to the contacts he made whilst he was there. In June, 1915 he notified his partners at Founders Court of his final decision to part company and his resignation took effect on 31 December that year. In his engagement book on that day (says Sir Henry Clay, in his biography of Lord Norman) he recorded these words: " A. H. B. and E. C. B. hail and farewell." (The reference is to Sir Alexander Hargreaves Brown and Edward Clifton Brown.)

It was during the summer of 1915 that Brown Brothers issued the first commercial export credit in dollars and in syndicate form, ever arranged. The war had greatly disturbed French exchange and the Bank of France sent a representative to the United States to discuss ways and means of stabilising it. After prolonged negotiation a commercial credit of 20 million dollars was arranged, secured by the deposit of French Treasury bills, payment in gold being guaranteed by the Bank of France. An additional credit of 25 million dollars was later issued on similar lines. For this unique service Browns were awarded a special medal and in an accompanying letter, signed by the Governor of the Bank of France, appreciation was expressed of the great service rendered by Brown Brothers at that critical time.

Early in the war and before the United States entered the war as a belligerent, the fact that Brown Brothers & Company and Brown, Shipley & Co. were one and the same concern, with every partner a partner in both firms, was already presenting many difficulties. War taxes, levied with increasing severity, and other difficulties made it impossible to maintain that complete fusion of interests that had characterised the two banks for over a century. At length, on January 1, 1918, formal notice was given of the ending of the partnership. Brown, Shipley & Co. withdrew from Brown Brothers & Company and the latter withdrew from Brown Shipley. Except for this

L

dissolution of partnership the two firms continued without any change in name or constitution, and each continued to act—though not exclusively—as agents of the other. Almost half a century has passed since that decision had to be taken, yet the ties that bound the two branches, though technically severed, have never been really broken.

Some years later, on 1 January, 1931, the name of the New York House of Brown Brothers & Company was changed in consequence of a merger with two other Banking Houses, viz: W. A. Harriman & Company Inc., and Harriman Bros. & Company. These two concerns had been founded by the brothers Harriman and the name of one of them—Mr. W. Averell Harriman—became even better known in this country during the Second World War. (He was appointed to this country by the United States Government to organise Lease/Lend activities, and later, after serving as U.S. Ambassador in Moscow, became American Ambassador in London.)

Following the American Banking Act of 1933 under which commercial banking and investment banking could no longer be undertaken by one and the same bank, the choice had to be made between the two, and Brown Brothers elected to continue as merchant bankers. Fully 65 per cent. of their business was concerned with the financing of exports and imports by commercial letters of credit, the receiving of deposits, granting of loans, and the buying and selling of foreign exchange; the remaining third of the firm's activities concerned underwriting and the selling of securities, and this section of the business was transferred, together with the security business of the National City Bank in New York, to a new and wholly independent Company styled Brown Harriman & Co. Inc., to which those partners concerned with the investment side transferred their interests. In 1938 the style or title of that Company was altered to Harriman Ripley & Co.

With the passing of the American Banking Act of 1933 the Baltimore house of Alex. Brown & Sons (the oldest firm of bankers in the United States) had also to make the choice between deposit banking and investment banking. Unlike Brown Brothers & Company (with whom Alex. Brown & Sons have had no financial connection since 1839) the Baltimore firm decided to concentrate on the securities and investment side of the business. Many families had been customers for three generations but (says Frank R. Kent, in his " History of Alex. Brown & Sons ") though the change was regrettable, " under the new conditions the securities business expanded, bringing even closer ties with customers seeking investment advice and service ".

The Brown Shipley—Brown Brothers partnership had survived wars and rumours of wars, and particularly the bad feeling between the two countries that was engendered by the American Civil War. It had also survived a series of grave financial crises on both sides of the Atlantic that had brought down many great firms in the banking world. The partnership was a unique example of Anglo-American co-operation. Behind it had always been a great tradition of integrity and fair dealing, laid down in the merchant venturing days by Alexander Brown. It was, however, inevitable in a changing world that the two banks should each go their separate ways, and although it marked the end of an era for Brown Shipley it has proved to be by no means the end of their story.

CHAPTER FOURTEEN

THE SECOND WORLD WAR

IF there were difficult days ahead for Brown Shipley they were also to be exciting ones. The dissolution of the interlocking partnership between the American and English Houses was a challenge that was gladly accepted. Up to that time, as has been seen, Brown Shipley's predominant interest had been in the North American continent, but the scope of the business was now broadened; indeed it is clear that, long before the actual break, the possibility of this occurring had in some measure been anticipated. One instance of this was the financing of Anglo-Russian oil projects; fortunately these had been brought to a successful conclusion long before the 1917 Russian Revolution. Apart from commercial credits, there had also been developments in the foreign exchange section of the business, and as far back as 1904 a separate Foreign Exchange department had been established and active dealings began in foreign exchange, both in the London Market and with Correspondent Bankers on the Continent. This quickly became a prominent activity at Founders Court and it is interesting to recall that the organiser of this department was a foreign exchange arbitrageur of wide experience named Robert Hecht. After six years at Founders Court he took up another appointment in the City. During the 1914-18 War he changed his name to Kay, and when Britain went off the Gold Standard in 1931 Robert Kay was appointed by the Bank of England as the first Manager of the Exchange Equalisation Fund. When (in 1921) the London Foreign Exchange Market was greatly enlarged, Brown, Shipley & Co. were able to secure a prominent place in it.

Before the 1914-18 War all acceptance business was conducted in sterling, and it was not until the upheaval caused by the war that Commercial Letters of Credit in dollars began to play a role of any importance in international trade. When the war had ended and Brown Shipley began to function as a separate bank, the competition of the U.S. commercial credits in dollars, by-passing London, and the consequent reduction in the volume of sterling credits coming forward from the U.S.A., were compensated by the ever-increasing acceptance business on U.K. account. As one City observer of the time put it: " Brown Shipley's American connection provides them with business in that sphere second to none, but they can in addition always obtain as much London business as they desire." The partners, however, were very conservative in their outlook. It was a changing world and conditions were very different to those that prevailed in 1914. The joint-stock banks had entered the field; so, too, had the foreign banks. It was a situation that called for enterprise and adaptability.

Two boom years had followed the Armistice and then came a fall in commodity prices from 325 per cent. (of pre-war level) in 1920, to 155 per cent. by the autumn of 1922. Imports were down from £1,710 million to £899 million in the same period, whilst the value of exports fell from £1,334 million to £720 million. Unemployment rose rapidly; from 7.8 per cent. in December, 1920 it had reached 17.7 per cent. a year later, and through the following years kept above 10 per cent. Alongside this depression at home, there were difficulties in America and, to an even greater extent, in continental countries where inflationary rises in prices and a weakening of exchanges took place. The Bank of England made urgent representations to all countries which had lapsed themselves from the Gold Standard that they should immediately return to it—not to the pre-war gold currency but to a " gold bullion " standard. Britain was ready to give a lead and, in due course, the Chancellor (Winston Churchill) in his Budget Speech in 1925 announced to the world Britain's return to the Gold Standard. Far from ending Britain's troubles it increased them. Its effect on the export trade was disastrous as we now had to face increased competition from countries like France, Italy and Belgium with undervalued currencies, and although by 1926 many countries had stabilised their currencies there was to be a continuous struggle to maintain sterling on gold—a struggle that finally ended in 1931 with the suspension of the Gold Standard. For Brown Shipley, as with all merchant banks, the rapid movements in the exchange value of sterling that resulted from this financial instability in the world, added greatly to their difficulties and posed many problems. Despite this, however, the firm succeeded in building up a very considerable credits business, particularly in the wool, timber, and fur trades.

Following the restoration of the Gold Standard in 1925 a great deal of short-term money was lent to Germany and used for capital investment. Unlike many of the merchant banks, some of which had close ties with Germany, Brown Shipley had few commitments there, and at the time of the credit crisis, when others found it impossible to get their money out of Germany and had to resort to the " Standstill " Agreement, Brown Shipley were fortunately involved only to a relatively minor extent.

Sir Alexander Hargreaves Brown died in 1922 at the age of 78. His son, Walter, had already joined the firm when the war ended, the partners at that time, in addition to Sir Alexander and his son, being Sir James Leigh-Wood, Edward Clifton-Brown, and Lawrence Chalmers. In 1921 Colonel Francis Edlmann was made a partner in Brown, Shipley & Co. Sir James Leigh-Wood retired from the firm in 1936.

When the Second World War broke out, in September,

1939, the experience gained in the 1914-18 War, when makeshift policies and organisation were inevitable, was reflected in the way the City markets were able to function. The Bank Rate, which had been raised to 4 per cent. in August, 1939, was reduced to 3 per cent. in September and to 2 per cent. in October, at which figure it remained until 1951. All necessary controls were applied, including Exchange Control, with the dollar at 4.02–4.06 to the £. The Stock Exchange was never closed, although minimum prices were fixed. As for merchant banking, by its very nature it could do little more than confine itself to routine business as both foreign exchange and commercial credits were, under war-time restrictions, greatly curtailed and confined to transactions approved by the Treasury. At Founders Court, despite the fact that most of the young men were serving in the Forces, the partners would have been justified in dispensing with the services of some of the staff, but they refused even to consider such a suggestion. All, however, were busy in their spare time, many serving as ambulance drivers, wardens, stretcher-bearers, or in the Home Guard, and many of the girls as nurses, canteen-workers, or in any capacity that could contribute to the war effort.

A letter from Brown, Shipley & Co. to one of the firm's Correspondents in Trinidad, early in 1941, gave an account of the conditions in London—the adaptability of the people; their cheerful acceptance of the grim conditions; their confidence in the outcome of the ordeal. A cable was received in reply that read as follows: —

" Deeply impressed . . . Completely contradicts several rumours circulating. Publication would greatly encourage and inspire community. May I?"

To this unexpected reaction Brown Shipley replied:

" By all means if you think advisable."

The letter had been brought to the notice of the Governor (Sir George Huggins) who said of it:

" It is not often that men like ourselves in this remote part of the world are privileged to receive such a letter from Banking interests . . . It gives a better view and understanding of what is taking place in England...and the confidence that inspires them to carry on should prompt us to do what we can to help them . . ."

Brown Shipley's letter was given wide publicity both in the Trinidad press and in support of the Fighter Fund and Bomber Fund the Governor was about to launch.

CHAPTER FIFTEEN

BROWN, SHIPLEY & CO. LIMITED

IF the First World War had posed new problems for Brown, Shipley & Co. they were nothing to those confronting the firm at the end of the Second World War. Until then it had been a private partnership, one of the few Merchant Banks to remain so. Moreover, since its foundation it had been almost entirely a family concern; but taxation and high death duties were making severe inroads into private fortunes and this at a time when the value of money was considerably reduced. The need for fresh capital, however, was not the sole problem. The days had gone when prestige alone was sufficient to keep Brown Shipley in the van of merchant banking; a new outlook was needed, preserving all that was best of the traditional family business, and equipping itself not only to meet the increasing competition of the joint-stock banks but to pioneer in new directions. Accordingly, in 1945, the firm decided on incorporation and on 1 January, 1946 its style or title became " Brown, Shipley & Co. Limited ".

Since then one of the most interesting developments at Founders Court has been the creation of a market in Foreign Notes to meet the needs of the two million or more tourists who go abroad each year and who spend not less than £100 million on foreign travel. Before the Second World War banks obtained direct whatever Notes their customers needed, and when the war began the foreign bank note market in London came virtually to an end. The main European dealings centred in Switzerland and remained there for some years after the war. By 1950 interest in foreign travel began to revive in this country when the travel allowance, which had hitherto been extremely small, and the currency allowance for other purposes smaller still, began gradually to be increased. The regulations governing the use of notes, both in foreign countries as well as here, were complicated and detailed. Specialisation was needed as a result of the growing number of countries that had imposed restrictions on their currencies, and Brown Shipley, with its world-wide connections, was able to build up a vast network abroad for the supply of foreign notes to other banks and to the travel agencies in this country. It thus created what is virtually a wholesale market in foreign notes in the City. By 1957 Brown Shipley were supplying foreign notes at the rate of some £20 million a year, and by the following year turnover had increased by 30 per cent. and continued to rise in the following years. No fewer than 125 different currencies are dealt in and it is not at all unusual for 50 or 60 of them to be handled on any one day. The firm trades in the notes with its Correspondents abroad, and dispatch to and from Founders Court is by air freight or post. In some dealings, however, the notes dealt with never even touch these shores.

Apart from the market in foreign notes the Foreign Exchange section of the bank has expanded. This, with the Commercial Credits department, which has never been more active than today, has been the mainstay of the firm since its foundation.

As an accepting house, Brown, Shipley & Co. are members of the Accepting Houses Committee. The Radcliffe Report has underlined the importance of accepting houses in the London money market and has stressed the fact that, in order to retain this power to accept bills of exchange, the bank has to satisfy the Bank of England that it has " adequate capital and adequate liquidity and that it is maintaining its reputation generally ". As nearly a quarter of all bills outstanding and almost half of the Bank bills are accounted for by accepting houses the volume of business is considerable. Brown Shipley's records show that, almost from the outset, the bank was providing Commercial Letters of Credit. There are very few trades and commodities with which they are not concerned, and they have been the means of helping to success a number of well-known firms in many fields.

Brown, Shipley & Co. afford borrowing facilities for financing all manner of business transactions. The bank also provides its customers with an Investment Advisory Service and (again quoting the Radcliffe Report) " this investment advisory service is something in which the accepting houses specialise to a far greater extent than other financial institutions." Brown Shipley have a complete Custody Service for customers and, in addition, maintain a Deposit Banking service for firms and individuals. With long-established correspondent relationships in almost every country, the bank is able to offer to its customers a really comprehensive banking service.

It was the deliberate policy of Alexander Brown, stressed over and over again in letters to his son William, to confine business alliances " *to the finest type and the most trustworthy of men* ", and it was a policy that has paid handsomely through the years. Brown, Shipley & Co. is proud of its great heritage and the tradition for reliability that has characterised the firm since its foundation. There is a story on record of a customer who, some years ago, was interviewing Sir Harry Thornton, at that time head of Canadian National Railways, in connection with a deal that was in prospect. Mention was made of Brown, Shipley & Co., to whom it was suggested Sir Harry should refer. On hearing this the latter retorted: " *That's quite unnecessary; the mere fact of your being a customer of Brown Shipley is sufficient reference.*"

The same spirit of great adventure which inspired William Brown a century and a half ago is still in evidence at Founders Court. There is, too, a feeling of enthusiasm and loyalty without which no Board of Directors could achieve success. May Brown, Shipley & Co, as the *" heir of adventure ",* long continue to go forward as *" the honour of credit ... the life of traffic and the maintenance of trade ... the pillar of a city, the enricher of a country ".*

APPENDIX

PARTNERS IN
WILLIAM BROWN & CO. (1810 – 1814)
WILLIAM & JAMES BROWN & CO. (1814 – 1837)
BROWN, SHIPLEY & CO. (1837 – 1945)
LIVERPOOL AND LONDON

WILLIAM BROWN - - - - - -	1810 – 1864
(Later Sir William Brown, Bart.)	
WILLIAM A. BROWN - - - - - -	1810 – 1812
GEORGE BROWN - - - - - -	1814 – 1839
JOHN A. BROWN - - - - - -	1814 – 1837
JAMES BROWN - - - - - - -	1814 – 1877
ELLISON FRODSHAM - - - - -	1816 – 1830
JOSEPH SHIPLEY - - - - - -	1826 – 1850
JOHN M. PRIESTMAN - - - - -	1830 – 1846
WILLIAM E. BOWEN - - - - -	1837 – 1859
SAMUEL NICHOLSON - - - - -	1838 – 1856
STEWART BROWN - - - - - -	1838 – 1880
FRANCIS ALEX. HAMILTON - - - -	1845 – 1903
MARK W. COLLET - - - - - -	1851 – 1905
(Later Sir Mark Collet, Bart.)	
STEWART HENRY BROWN - - - -	1856 – 1888
HERMAN HOSKIER - - - - -	1866 – 1880
FREDERICK CHALMERS - - - - -	1869 – 1898
ALEX. HARGREAVES BROWN - - - -	1875 – 1920
(Later Sir Alex. Hargreaves Brown, Bart.)	
LAWRENCE EDLMANN CHALMERS - - -	1898 – 1924
EDWARD CLIFTON-BROWN - - - - -	1899 – 1944
MONTAGU C. NORMAN - - - - -	1900 – 1915
(Later Lord Norman)	
J. LEIGH WOOD - - - - - - -	1907 – 1936
(Later Sir J. Leigh-Wood)	
WALTER HARGREAVES BROWN - - - -	1915 – 1936
FRANCIS J. F. EDLMANN - - - - -	1921 – 1945
JOHN G. W. HUSTED - - - - -	1930 – 1939
ANTHONY G. CLIFTON-BROWN - - - -	1935 – 1945
ROGER LEIGH-WOOD - - - - - -	1937 – 1942

NOTE: Until 1st January, 1918 all Partners in the American firm were also Partners in the English firm.

DIRECTORS OF BROWN, SHIPLEY & CO.
LIMITED

Francis J. F. Edlmann - - - - - 1946 – 1950

Anthony G. Clifton-Brown - - - - 1946 – 1953

Angus Mackinnon - - - - - - 1946 –

Ion Garnett-Orme* - - - - - 1946 –

Leslie Ingram Chester - - - - - 1948 – 1957

Sir Giles Guthrie, Bart. - - - - - 1949 –

George Ronald Tobitt - - - - - 1956 –

The Rt. Hon. Lord Farnham - - - - 1959 –

* Descendant of William Brown.

INDEX

INDEX

Trans-Siberian Railway, 133.
Trent, 73; 80-84.
Trinidad, Correspondents in, 151; 152.

Union Court, Liverpool, 25.
United States Bank, 22; 24; 27.
U.S. Commercial Credits, 149.

War of 1812, 9; 10; 13; 16; 89; 90.
West End Office of Brown, Shipley & Co., 130-138.
Westminster Bank, 44; 134.
West Virginia Debt, 127.
Wiggin, Timothy & Co., 36; 57.
Wilder, George & Co., 36; 57.
William Brown, 54; 59; *illus. facing p. 60.*
Wilmington, Delaware, 56.
Wilson, Thomas & Co., 36; 56; 57.
Winans, Ross, 133.
Winans, Thomas & William J., 133.
Wood, James Leigh, 139; 150.
Workman, W. Hunter, 138.
World War I, 139-145.
" W's ", The Three, 36; 41; 49; 57.